A STUDENT'S GUIDE
TO SURVIVING
AND THRIVING IN
ONLINE CLASSES

A STUDENT'S GUIDE TO SURVIVING AND THRIVING IN ONLINE CLASSES

Richard D. Parsons

cognella® | ACADEMIC PUBLISHING

Bassim Hamadeh, CEO and Publisher
Amy Smith, Senior Project Editor
Abbey Hastings, Production Editor
Emely Villavicencio, Senior Graphic Designer
Alexa Lucido, Licensing Manager
Natalie Piccotti, Director of Marketing
Kassie Graves, Vice President of Editorial
Jamie Giganti, Director of Academic Publishing

Cover image: Copyright © 2019 iStockphoto LP/Eva-Katalin.

Printed in the United States of America.

THE COGNELLA SERIES ON STUDENT SUCCESS

S tudent success isn't always measured in straight As.

Many students arrive at college believing that if they study hard and earn top grades, their higher education experience will be a success. Few recognize that some of their greatest learning opportunities will take place outside the classroom. Learning how to manage stress, navigate new relationships, or put together a budget can be just as important as acing a pop quiz.

The Cognella Series on Student Success is a collection of books designed to help students develop the essential life and learning skills needed to support a happy, healthy, and productive higher education experience. Featuring topics suggested by students and books written by experts, the series offers research-based, yet practical advice to help any student navigate new challenges and succeed throughout their college experience.

Series Editor: Richard Parsons, Ph.D.
Professor of Counselor Education, West Chester University

Other titles available in the series:

- *A Student's Guide to Stress Management*
- *A Student's Guide to a Meaningful Career*
- *A Student's Guide to College Transition*
- *A Student's Guide to Money Matters*
- *A Student's Guide to Communication and Self-Presentation*
- *A Student's Guide to Exercise for Improving Health*

BRIEF CONTENTS

DETAILED CONTENTS

EDITOR'S PREFACE

The transition to college marks a significant milestone in a person's life. Many of you will be preparing to live away from your friends and family for the very first time. Clearly this is should be an exciting time.

It is a time to experience new things and experiment with new options. While the opportunity to grow is clear, so are the many challenges you will experience as you transition from high school to college.

Research suggests that the first year of college is the most difficult period of adjustment a student faces. Not only will you be required to adjust to new academic demands, but you will also have to navigate a number of social and emotional challenges that accompany your life as a college student. The books found within this series—*Cognella Series on Student Success*—have been developed to help you with the many issues confronting your successful transition from life as a high school student to life as a collegiate. Each book within the series was designed to provide research-based yet *practical* advice to help you succeed in your college experience.

Richard Parsons, Ph.D.
Series Editor

AUTHOR'S PREFACE

Let's do a little mind experiment with some free association. What comes to mind when you hear "online course"?

Do you imagine yourself in your jammies? Perhaps you envision taking your classes in bed with snacks. Maybe the thought of online courses just stimulates a sense of flexibility and freedom. If these are connections you make when you think of an online course, you probably are correct, at least with the concept of flexibility.

There are many advantages to taking an online course, but there are also a number of unique challenges. By definition, online courses require a degree of technical sophistication. Online courses have less, if any, physical contact with instructor or classmates. Online courses will require more self discipline, time management, and task management than typically required by a traditional brick-and-mortar classroom experience.

Online programs and courses can positively contribute to your educational experience and your professional development. The other side of this coin is that online courses, by the very nature of their designs, will place demands on you, the learner, that are different than those you may have encountered when taking a live, on-campus course.

This book, *A Student's Guide To Surviving and Thriving in Online Classes*, provides you with practical, researched-based suggestions to help you not only survive but actually thrive in an online educational experience. As you review the material you will soon come to appreciate that the strategies offered to assist your online experience will not only serve you well with your online course(s) but will serve you well as you follow your path toward a successful career.

"This is so … unfair!"

That sentiment was made by Maddie, a soon to be Division I athlete and chemistry major. Her move to campus has been placed on hold, all as a result of COVID-19. Perhaps you can relate?

For many students, the excitement generated with the opening of a letter of acceptance and the anticipation of a new experience, away from home, came crashing down with the introduction of COVID-19. COVID-19 has disrupted life as we expected it to be.

Remaining at home with online classes may not have been your choice. At the present time, however, it may be your only option. This will not be the case forever. So, it is vital that you make the most of it.

The current text, *A Student's Guide to Surviving and Thriving in Online Classes*, will help you structure your learning experiences, maintain your motivation, and effectively manage your tasks and time. These are all valuable skills—for online or on-campus learning.

RP/July 2020

NOT YOUR GRANDFATHER'S CLASSROOM

I f you are reading this book, it is very likely that you are taking or considering taking an online course. If so ... you are not alone.

It has been predicted that the majority of all higher education students will take at least one online course during their educational experience (Babson, 2014). According to the National Center for Education Statistics (2014), over 5.4 million students in 2012 were engaged in at least one online course. These data, which are the latest, while dated, suggest that the trend is toward increased online curriculum because of the number of advantages these courses offer.

1.1: An Attractive Alternative ... For Some

Online courses are generally very convenient: a student does not need to be overly concerned about dress, transportation, or dealing with bad weather. Online courses offer a higher degree of flexibility in that they allow students to decide, to some degree, when, where, and how quickly (the pace) the material will be addressed.

A student, for example, might engage with the content for most of one day, even to return at night to fine-tune their work. Or, perhaps, that same student may decide that today is not a good day to sit at the computer and may choose instead to spend the day outdoors or at a job. If you find that your motivation, your "get up and go," has "gotten up and gone," then, unless there are strict requirements for meeting online at specific times, the online course will allow you to adjust the schedule to maximize your achievement.

Having the freedom to step in, step out, and step back in again at the times it will be most beneficial and productive can be a real benefit of online classes. This flexibility will not only contribute to your comfort but also allows for maximum opportunity for growth and academic achievement.

The freedom and flexibility provided by an online course extends beyond the scheduling of time and day. Online courses allow for freedom and flexibility in terms of selecting the context and setting in which you choose to engage with the learning materials. This can be seen as a real benefit, especially for students who would rather not have to sit for a designated length of time in a crowded lecture hall. The freedom and flexibility that characterizes online courses is often the primary reason students engage with online programs. There are other benefits of online courses when compared to the more traditional brick-and-mortar, on-campus courses. Perhaps, before reading what others have identified as benefits, you could take a moment to reflect upon your own expectations so as to contrast those found by others (see Exercise 1.1).

EXERCISE 1.1

What I See as Benefits to Online Courses

Directions: Research, both anecdotal and empirical, has identified student- and faculty-identified benefits to online course delivery. As you begin your online experience, it would be helpful to take a moment to reflect on the following. Identifying what you anticipate as benefits to an online experience will help you consider the best ways to structure and engage in the course so as to experience these benefits.

1. How will the flexibility of when, where, and how you engage in the course work for you?

2. How might the ability to do your work in isolation from a class of peers be a benefit?

3. What economic benefits (e.g., travel costs) might you experience?

4. Given the emphasis on self-directed learning, how might an online course contribute to your overall growth and development (beyond the specific knowledge or skills you may develop)?

Having a Life Even When in College

Your college courses and degree program have probably taken center stage in your current life activities. Even with this prioritization of your education, the reality is that you do or should have a life outside of school. With online courses, you can work and fit your work schedule (and your hobbies) around your coursework more efficiently. This is especially true if the class is an asynchronous online class. With an asynchronous class you are not required to log in at a specific time for a live class. You can study and interact with your instructor and your fellow classmates at your own pace through, for example, the discussion forum.

Being able to choose the when and where of your engagement with the learning materials provides you the freedom to integrate school with other life demands (e.g., work, appointments, chores) or interests (e.g., hobbies, friends, exercise). Being in college, while demanding, should not require you to place life outside of academics on hold. All work and no play makes you-know-who a dull person. Online courses allow for such an integrated and rounded life experience.

Comfortable Learning Environment

If you go online and check some of the university websites advertising their online programs and courses, it is a safe bet you will see at least one picture of a student in pajamas engaging with an online class. I am not suggesting pajamas should be the uniform for online courses. In fact, you will see later in this text reasons why that may not be a good idea. What I am suggesting is that online courses will allow you to create a learning setting and environment that not only contributes to your comfort, but optimizes your ability to focus and engage in the learning materials.

With online courses, the options for settings and contexts are varied. The classroom could be your bedroom, your study, the coffee shop down the street, or even your gym (if you are listening to a lecture). As will be discussed in the upcoming chapters, developing a setting, a context, and an actual physical environment that is comfortable is essential. However, it is not just comfort that is desired. Your decision about the setting or context for your online course engagement should also be supportive of your learning style (see Chapter 3) and thus maximally conducive to your learning. Take a moment for a little mind experiment (see Exercise 1.2).

EXERCISE 1.2

Comfort and Conducive

Directions: You get the picture. You want to be in a setting that you find comfortable. Still, not all comfortable environments (think hot shower) are conducive to learning. So take a moment to do a little free association followed by some critical thinking.

In the first column, you will find a list of settings or characteristics of an environment. From your perspective, would you consider them comfortable? Conducive to learning? Both? Neither? List your answer in the second column. Now review each of your answers and find ways, if possible, to make the less-than-comfortable settings that are conducive more comfy, and the comfy settings more conducive.

Setting	Comfy (CY), Conducive (CL), Both (B), Neither (N)	Creative ways to increase the comfy/conducive factor
Bed … with comforter		
Local pub		
Library		
Gym		
Kitchen table		
Living room or family room		
At a desk		
At the park, backyard … simply outside		
(other) what one spot would maximize your comfort and your ability to achieve academically	(BOTH)	(ideas to increase even this setting's value?)

So, back to the PJ's. Comfortable? Yes. Conducive to learning? I guess that one will be dependent on other factors—factors which we consider later in the book (see Chapter 3). For now, the message is COMFORT … in service of LEARNING!

Down with Commuting

Taking an online course also means that you don't have to commute to class—except for the commute from your bed to your desk.

Think about that. Cost savings in terms of gas or transportation fees and less time spent traveling and fighting the elements or even circling the parking lot anxiously looking for a spot. Have you experienced anxiety about running late for class, especially if a test was scheduled? How about on those days of iced-over roads? With online courses, these points of stress and anxiety are reduced. The change in venue should help remove some of the stress or at least inconvenience often encountered commuting to class, even when that commute is from dorm to classroom.

Giving Room for My "Voice"

There are students who are somewhat introverted or shy or may simply be the type of student that prefers to take a little time to reflect on an instructor's question or observation before responding. If you are such a reflective learner, then you can appreciate the value of having time to digest material in order to make cognitive connections before speaking up in class or engaging in a classroom discussion. Such reflection is often not possible if participating in a classroom with a number of spontaneous and active responders.

For students with a reflective style of learning, sitting in a large lecture hall—where one almost needs to "fight" for recognition or compete with a lot of very active, spontaneous, and assertive students—may be less than conducive to their learning. These students find that the freedom and opportunity to share their voice by way of emails, texts, message boards, and drop-boxes not only encourages them to contribute but facilitates their ability to actively participate.

1.2: Challenges

Online courses do offer numerous benefits that are not typically found in the traditional, brick-and-mortar class delivery model. But online courses are not without some challenges and potential costs. In fact, for some students, online courses may prove to be a significant challenge to their learning and their ability to demonstrate that learning.

Confused

With an online format it is possible that you may be a bit confused or unclear about the specific nature of the course requirements or assignments or even some of the content that may be presented. Misunderstandings that could readily be rectified in a face-to-face encounter with the instructor may now need to be clarified through less-than-desirable modes of communication (e.g., texts, postings).

Tech

Online courses require technology, both hardware and software, which could present challenges for students with limited technology expertise or comfort. Further, the simple fact of needing to rely on the functionality of the technology may invite added stress and frustration—given that power outages can and do occur and "bugs" are to be expected.

Self-Discipline

The freedom and flexibility offered by an online experience can be beneficial; however, for these factors to be maximally contributory to your education and academic success, you will have to exert self-discipline and self-direction. With online classes, the primary responsibility for engaging and maintaining achievement motivations falls to you, the student. You will have to activate your own motivation, either intrinsic or extrinsic, and use the self-regulation skills necessary for success. Lack of ongoing motivation can result in a student losing sight of the original goal and failing to maintain progress and momentum (Chaney, 2001).

It would appear that students who have a tendency or history of relying heavily on others prodding, poking, and reminding them may find the freedom and flexibility of an online course more costly than beneficial. Similarly, students who find themselves easily distracted or disorganized in their approaches to learning and who place more value on non-class opportunities and experiences than those presented within the course may not be well suited for online courses. Finally, the freedom and flexibility celebrated as a payoff of the online format can also present a significant challenge to those students who are prone to procrastination.

For many students, especially those who are enrolled in an online course for the first time, the need to be self-disciplined and remain motivated in the absence of the instructor's face-to-face encouragement can be quite a challenge. The chapters that follow will help you strengthen your abilities to become just such an independent, self-directed learner.

These and other conditions (see Table 1.1) can be challenges and may contribute additional levels of frustration and stress, resulting in less-than-desirable grades.

Table 1.1. Perceived Advantages and Disadvantages of Online Courses

Advantages	Disadvantages
• Convenience (dress, travel) • Flexibility (time, pace) • Don't have to sit through classroom lectures • Ability to view/review lecture videos as needed • Lower costs (parking, food) • Less stress (to be on time, find parking) • Don't have to deal with other students disrupting class • Don't have to wait for other students who work at a slower pace • Don't have to work in class teams	• More likely to procrastinate • Harder to understand content when not face-to-face with instructor • Requires more self-discipline for reading and learning • More likely to misunderstand directions • More stressful trying to reach instructor when help is needed • More stress related to technology issues • More computer-related distractions (Facebook, etc.)

Adapted from "Expected Advantages and Disadvantages of Online Learning,"
by M. W. Alexander, A. D. Truell, & J. J. Zhao, 2012, Issues in Information Systems,
13(2), pp. 193–200.

1.3: Don't Surrender: Maximizing Benefits/Decreasing Costs

The freedom and flexibility afforded with an online course places much of the responsibility on the student. To be successful with an online course, you will have to be self-regulating—able to plan, monitor, evaluate, and then adjust your own behavior, cognition, and learning strategies (Matuga, 2009; You & Kang, 2014)

The curriculum has been structured by the instructor, as have the assignments, the tasks, and the measures of performance; however, the method of delivery invites each student to set personal goals, maintain interest and motivation, and monitor progress and momentum. Given the nature of online courses, success will not only be contingent upon the student's intellectual abilities but also their ability to be self-motivating, organized, and efficient at time management.

The good news is that not only can these skills be developed, but the very process of engaging in online courses can serve as the learning opportunity for just such development. As might be obvious, these skills and dispositions will not only serve you well with a specific online course but will be valuable assets as you move on to other classes and eventually on to a career.

1.4: It Starts with Taking Stock

Even if you feel that you may be a less-than-ideal candidate for thriving in an online environment, do not despair. The elements necessary to prove successful are elements that can be learned, embraced, and enacted by each of us.

The remaining chapters address these issues and the steps you can take to become a self-regulated learner and experience success with online courses. The process, however, starts with a little self-analysis—taking stock of your own unique strengths and challenges as they may come to bear on your success with online learning.

Exercise 1.3 invites you to take time for a little honest self-reflection and personal assessment. The data you collect will help guide you toward not only surviving but thriving in an online course.

EXERCISE 1.3

Time to Take Account

You have reviewed some of the benefits and potential challenges encountered when taking an online course. It is helpful to spend a moment to reflect on those factors that excite or perhaps energize you about taking an online course. It is also of value to reflect upon the elements or conditions presented with online learning that may be a challenge to your ultimate success.

Identifying these areas of difficulty will help focus your attention on the upcoming chapters and the specific ways the information presented will help you reduce those challenges and maximize your gains.

What's in it for me? What is the payoff/desired outcome that I am aiming for?	List specific payoffs.	Develop a strategy for maximizing that payoff.
	(1)	
	(2)	
	(3)	
Reflecting on my previous style as a student and approach to learning—what strengths and talents do I bring to this online experience that will help me attain my goals?		
	(1)	
	(2)	
	(3)	
What are the barriers to my maintenance of motivation?	List specific challenges or barriers to your online success.	Develop a strategy to remove or minimize these barriers.
	(1)	
	(2)	
	(3)	
What elements in my life may be distracting or competing for my time and energy?		
	(1)	
	(2)	
	(3)	
What behavior or style as a student have I exhibited in the past that could be a barrier to my online success?		
	(1)	
	(2)	
	(3)	

REFRAMING YOUR CONCEPT OF THE "CLASSROOM"

Your online course may be held in one room, but it is not the one room of a brick-and-mortar schoolhouse. Going to class, when online, will undoubtedly be different than what you have experienced during your years of schooling.

Whether you realize it or not, you have been socialized ... make that "schoolized" ... to step into a mindset as well as a repertoire of behaviors all cued by sight, sounds, and even the smells of a school and a classroom. Perhaps you, like me, retain strong memories of the smell of the cleaning supplies used in your elementary school, or the whiff of the middle school cafeteria, or the feel of sitting in your high school auditorium. These sensory memories were imprinted over years of experience, and each one truly acts as an unconscious guide to remind you where you are and what you should anticipate. In other words, the conditions of the school and the classroom help to place you in the mindset necessary for acting like a student.

The almost predictable elements found within a brick-and-mortar classroom are designed to facilitate the learning process. Take a moment to reflect on your previous experience with the traditional school and classroom. It is fair to assume that you went to a specific classroom and you most likely had an assigned seat—or at least an area that you typically used to do your work. There was a teacher who not only structured but directed the learning activities—keeping you on task, or at least trying to keep you on task. And, of course, there was a clear beginning and a defined ending to the class or school day, often marked by a bell, a buzzer, or an announcement. While the details of any one classroom will vary, it is safe to assume that each of the above descriptors applies to most traditional classrooms.

2.1: More Than Decorations

When we think of the various sensory experiences that are somewhat commonplace to our schooling experience (especially during the elementary years), we may simply attempt to dismiss them as "interesting," "nice," or perhaps even curious. But the reality is that these stimuli have developed into cues or triggers that can elicit certain expectations, feelings, and behaviors.

If you had the opportunity to revisit one of your elementary or middle school classrooms you might be surprised to find that, at least for a brief moment, you are swept back to those early days of your education. You may, even momentarily, feel like that third-grade or seventh-grade you.

For anyone like me who may have been a less-than-model student, stepping back into that environment may even arouse a bit of anxiety. Similarly, for those for whom much about school was positive, exciting, and personally satisfying, the re-experiencing of the familiar sensory input of those days gone by can elicit strong positive feelings. The physical and social cues that we have come to associate with school have the power of eliciting specific attitudes and expectations (mindsets) as well as behaviors. Learning mindsets are a set of beliefs that are linked to academic performance in students and affect how we engage with challenges, initiate and self-direct our learning, and even set the stage for how we interpret our day-to-day experiences in school, particularly experiences of adversity.

Consider the example of two students who receive the same exact low score on a project but who, because of the mindsets and attitudes they developed about self and school, come to significantly different conclusions and reactions. A student who sees herself as less than capable or believes that school is too hard or irrelevant may not only surrender in the face of this task but may attempt to avoid similar challenges in the future—motivated by the drive to avoid failure. Whereas a student with a sense of self-efficacy (believing she has the ability) may view a low grade as an indication that she simply hasn't mastered the material yet. As a result, she may increase her efforts, ask for help, and try different strategies.

A person's mindset can determine how he or she approaches challenges, responds to criticism, and perceives his or her self-worth (Dweck, 2006). When the conditions of school stimulate your growth mindset, you will find yourself excited about the possibility of stretching yourself and sticking to it even (or especially) when it's not going well. A positive growth mindset is often elicited when a classroom teacher models enthusiasm and positive expectations while encouraging the students to do the same. With online courses, the engagement of a positive mindset is primarily up to you.

Our mindsets about school, learning, and ourselves as students not only affect our attitude and expectations, but serve to direct our behaviors in response to school demands. When our perspective, attitude, or mindset about learning is positive, the various stimuli that have become associated with schooling elicit productive and appropriate learning behaviors.

If you found school to be an exciting place where your curiosity was stimulated and your desire to initiate and direct your learning was encouraged and supported, then boy are you fortunate. This attitude, these behaviors of initiation and self-directed learning, will serve you well.

However, if some of your previous experience in a classroom was less than ideal, there is a good chance that you may have developed behaviors which, while easing the discomfort at the moment, may serve as a barrier to your academic achievement. In this situation, being successful will require you to not only focus on the content of the course, but on developing and maintaining the positive mindsets and productive behaviors shown to facilitate academic achievement.

Table 2.1 provides a sample of the types of mindsets and behaviors that have been found to facilitate academic achievement. Working on the development of these positive mindsets and behaviors will serve you well in this course and in all of life's challenges.

Table 2.1. Mindsets and Behaviors that Facilitate Learning

Mindset	Behaviors
I believe in my abilities to succeed.	I appear eager, excited, and energized when starting a new course, a new unit, or a new task.
It is safe to risk.	I ask questions or offer answers.
I can and do initiate.	I set goals and time lines for achieving those goals.
I am optimistic and hopeful when it comes to school tasks.	I employ evaluation and feedback to guide my next steps.
I am flexible when running into a problem or a roadblock.	I take breaks, walk away, and then come back to tasks that I am having some difficulty completing.
I am resilient. I bounce back from disappointments or setbacks.	Even after a disappointment I get up and start all over again.
I am persistent. I keep attacking even when something is challenging.	Once I'm into something I work to see it to completion.
I am empathic. I care about how others feel and can imagine what it is like to be in their position.	I support others and seek support from them.
I see school and my education as having purpose, value, and relevance.	I keep my eye on the prize. I have a clear goal, and I measure my progress in school as a means to move me toward that goal.
I feel like I am valued and respected by my teachers and peers.	I seek feedback as opportunities for growth.

Since the positive mindsets and behaviors you have developed about yourself as a student and your approach to school will facilitate your engagement as an active, interested, and motivated student, they will need to be activated as you engage with your online course. The challenge is that the cues you have gleaned from your experiences with brick-and-mortar classrooms, those cues that can elicit the positive mindsets and behaviors, are absent with your online experience.

The challenge therefore will be to reclaim the elements that engage your positive mindset and facilitate your academic achievement. When this is not possible (you can't re-create the wonderful smell of chemistry class) you will need to find alternative ways to address the needs serviced by those elements.

The suggestion is not to build a classroom replica at home; instead, the idea is to find out how these elements facilitated learning and find alternative ways to introduce similar facilitative features into your own online experience.

2.2: The Classroom—A Physical Space

Classrooms are complex environments in which people interact interdependently with one another and with the unique characteristics of the specific physical space and social dynamic. Those within the classroom are interacting and affecting one another ... and they are affected by their surroundings.

When we consider the physical environment of a classroom, we are taking into consideration the overall design, layout, and appointments of the classroom. We know, for example, that the color of paint, the type of lighting, the decorations, and most certainly the type and arrangement of desks can have a significant impact on the kind of learning activities provided and the degree to which students feel engaged and become active learners. Exercise 2.1 invites you to take a moment and identify the types of physical elements in a classroom that seem to make your learning more or less enjoyable and more or less productive. The features that you identify can be combined with those discussed in Chapter 3 (Learning Styles) in order to help you develop a physical space that is most conducive to your academic achievement.

EXERCISE 2.1

The Physical Environment of the Classroom

Directions: Below you will see a list of physical characteristics often found in a brick-and-mortar classroom. Your task is to identify those characteristics that seem to contribute to your active learning and those which can be somewhat inhibiting.

Element	Contributes to active and successful learning	Seems to negatively impact my energy, my enthusiasm, my academic achievement	Ideas about using this element in my online classroom	Ideas about removing or avoiding the inclusion of this element in my online classroom
Tight space (crowded—small)				
Limited mobility (due to seating or some other physical element)				
Bright lights				
Subdued lighting				
Quiet—like in a library				
Visibility				
Visual prompts— posters, notes				
Seat type and comfort				
Seating configuration (rows, horseshoe, amphitheater, etc.)				
(other physical characteristics you remember)				

2.3: The Classroom—A Social Environment

A second characteristic of a traditional brick-and-mortar class is that it is also a "social environment." A classroom is not merely a collection of desks, whiteboards, and learning materials. A classroom is "peopled" and is thus a social as well as physical environment. Composed of individuals gathered for the common purpose of learning that which is to be presented, with varying degrees of interaction and mutual engagement, each classroom is a unique social environment exhibiting a unique social dynamic. While this may appear to be a simple artifact of having a teacher and students in the same locale, a condition without real significance, research has consistently shown that academic achievement is correlated with high levels of group support and cooperation. Research demonstrates that learning can be maximized when classrooms are not merely social settings but evolve into a place where members feel connected as a community of learners. Thus, one of the most useful things a teacher can achieve is the creation of a classroom filled with interactive, interdependent groups of learners.

A robust online learning community keeps students engaged with the content, pushes them to think critically and articulate their ideas, and provides a supportive environment in which to do that. The concept of a community of learners recognizes that students are an essential source of knowledge, which, in combination with course material and faculty insights, can provide a vibrant learning experience. But to tap students as a resource, conditions must exist that invite their engagement. For a learning community to be effective, students will need to be engaged in reciprocal learning activities—sharing ideas, experiences, perspectives, and insights.

The physical separation that characterizes an online course makes the creation of such a community of learners challenging … but not impossible. Instructors of online courses will hopefully engage students in a way that fosters interaction and interdependence. A course may require live interaction via a platform such as Zoom or interactive and interdependent projects and assignments. When building a sense of community among the students, many instructors will employ discussion boards, collaborative projects, wikis, blogs, and real-time (synchronous) sessions.

2.4: It May Be Up to You

The creation of an online learning community can facilitate academic achievement and make for a more personally satisfying experience. Your participation as a member of a learning community will encourage you to initiate, respect, value, and fully engage in the material, dialogues, and group work.

The results of this are academic success and personal satisfaction. Without such interaction and sense of community, it is easy to feel isolated.

Many online courses have been designed in a way that offers the physical and social environments known to facilitate learning. But what happens when the social structures or engaging elements are not incorporated into an online class? What happens if it genuinely is left up to me?

Under these conditions, then, it is incumbent on you to make as much of a learning community and supportive network as possible. At a minimum, this means that you must risk reaching out and connecting with the others in your course. It will be through shared discussion, reflection, and often just by merely listening to others that a cohesive group, a learning community, can begin to take form.

One specific way that this cohesiveness can be fostered is by interacting with your peers around specific task goals. If you and others in the course can identify things that you are working on (tasks involved with the course completion) and set up a mechanism for sharing ideas as well as supporting and challenging one another, then you will find that cohesiveness and "we-ness" begins to take shape. Now, when the structure of the course does not allow for such interdependence or interaction around the tasks of the course, cohesiveness can still be fostered by coming together around social-emotional goals (i.e., providing messages of acceptance, encouragement, and support to one another).

Additional things that you can do to provide and receive social support and a sense of belonging when engaged with an online course include the following:

1. *Be available*. It can be frustrating at times when connections are not smooth or responses are delayed, but the more you reach out to the professor AND to your peers, the more connections and community are made.

2. *Establish a communication plan*. Set up a calendar to remind you to check in with the professor and with your classmates. Show them that you care and are interested in them, and this care and interest will be returned in kind.

3. *React, respond, interact*. Yes, you will be busy. You have your own work to complete, but it is important to engage in communal

discussion boards, respond to peer presentations, and invite reactions to your work.

4. _More than academics_. When building a community, it helps to share—as appropriate—your "non-school self." If you were in a brick-and-mortar class, you might engage with classmates at the café or coffee shop. You may share your experience with a movie or a sporting event. Find time before or after "class" to engage your peers. Deliberately creating such moments fosters the development of a safe, trusting climate.

Exercise 2.2 invites you to consider your past social experience with brick-and-mortar classes as it may reflect belonging to a learning community. The task is to identify elements that may have contributed to the development of a supportive social environment.

As you engage with your online course, you will find that the inclusion of these same elements, as much as possible, will foster the development of a community of learners and help you to maintain motivation, stay involved, and remain task-focused—this will enhance your academic achievement.

EXERCISE 2.2

Developing a Community of Learners

Directions: Identify two of your most recent brick-and-mortar class experiences. Attempt to identify a class in which there was very little peer-to-peer interaction or sense of a singular learning community or group. This would be a class where you felt (as did others) that it was "everyone for themselves." Now identify a class in which you felt a sense of camaraderie with your classmates. It was a class where you experienced the development of a real sense of working together and being a learning community—you felt that learning was occurring student-to-student as well as teacher-to-student. With these two classes in mind, identify elements that fostered or inhibited the development of a learning community. As you create the social environment for your online course, you will want to incorporate as many of the features that contributed to the formation of a learning community while at the same time removing or reducing those that were inhibitory.

Characteristic	Low level of community of learners—elements that inhibited the development of a learning community	Higher level of group identity and learning community—elements that fostered the development of a learning community	My ideas for creating a learning community in my online course
Open communications			
Degree of student-to-student interactions/teaching			
Climate of "safety" (can ask or answer questions without concern for adverse reactions from teacher or peers)			
Climate of "curiosity" (questions were encouraged and valued)			
Climate of "support" (student participation was encouraged by faculty/peer praise)			
Sense of camaraderie—the students felt they were "all in this together"			
An environment of intense competition—student against student for recognition or grades			
A sense of shared goals and purpose			
A climate of valuing and helping one another—sharing			
A sense of mutual commitment			
A trusting environment			

LEARNING STYLE

PREFERRED WAY OF ACQUIRING, PROCESSING, AND RETAINING INFORMATION

The term "learning styles" describes an individual's preferred way of acquiring, processing, and retaining information. Your preferred learning style is how YOU learn best. For example, let's assume you purchased a piece of furniture that required assembly. You open the box, and you find very detailed written assembly instructions. The manufacturer even included step-by-step pictures of the piece being assembled. The question is … do you read the detailed description or do you simply attempt to follow the illustrations … or do you just start picking up pieces and seeing what goes with what (at least in your mind)?

Some individuals would review the written instructions and follow them very methodically, taking each step one at a time. Others may prefer viewing the diagrams and sketches. Then there are others—like me—who are more impulsive and dive in attaching pieces that "intuitively" appear to go together. The idea isn't that one way—be that reading instructions, processing visual images, or handling the materials—is the best way; the focus is on which of these approaches, if any, works best for the individual. That would be an indication of their preferred learning style.

There is research that would suggest that our learning styles, while being influenced by our previous experience, are actually hardwired into our physical/neurological makeup. As such, it would appear that rather than attempting to change your learning style preference, it would be better to identify the conditions of preferred learning styles and adapt the learning environment and approach so that you can engage the learning material in ways that most closely align with your learning style. To do this you need to begin to identify your own learning style.

3.1: VAKT It!

There are numerous approaches to the depiction of those characteristics that distinguish one's learning style. One model presented by Neil Fleming, an educational theorist, posits that learning styles fall into three categories: visual learners, auditory learners, and kinesthetic (and tactile) learners (Fleming & Baume, 2006). These are not exclusive categories. An individual can process information through each or any of these channels. However, it is very likely that you find learning and information processing more effective when the material is presented visually (e.g., think PowerPoint or movies), in an auditory form (e.g., lecture or books on tape), in a hands-on format where you can move about (e.g., dance, visual arts), or when the material can be manipulated (e.g., engineering or structural models). It is possible that you cannot narrow your preference to one modality over another—you may experience more effective learning when engaged through multiple modalities. Take a moment and consider the questions posed in Exercise 3.1 as they may begin to help you identify your VAKT preference.

EXERCISE 3.1

What's Your VAKT?

Directions: Take a moment to think about times and situations in class when you felt most engaged or had the most difficulty staying focused. Again, there may not be a clear "winner," but let's see how your profile may unfold. Your task is to complete the following chart.

(Additional learning style inventories are listed in the appendix and can be accessed online.)

Modality	Description	The degree to which this seems best for you (1 = yuk; 10 = perfecto)	Suggestion for maximizing
Visual learner	"Give me a class or textbook that has lots of images, maps, graphic organizers." Do you do best in classes in which teachers do a lot of writing at the chalkboard, provide clear handouts, and make extensive use of an overhead projector? Do you try to remember information by creating pictures in your mind? Do you take detailed written notes from your textbooks and in class? If YES, you are probably a visual learner.		• Create graphic organizers such as charts and diagrams. • Use a three-column approach to note-taking: first write out your narrative, in the next, reduce the long description to a set of phrases, in the last column reduce the phrases to a set of "letters" or symbols almost like you may create as a reminder card. • Use a highlighter and, if possible, color code similar concepts or terms. • Use color, thoughtful layouts, and well-chosen fonts to help retain information. • Organize notes via color coordination and incorporate pictures and images in review sessions.

(Continued)

Modality	Description	The degree to which this seems best for you (1 = yuk; 10 = perfecto)	Suggestion for maximizing
Auditory learner	"Give me a book on tape! I love to listen to a 'good' speaker and engage in group discussions." Do you seem to learn best in classes that emphasize teacher lectures and class discussions? Can you attend to a professor's lecture without looking at the instructor? Does listening to audio tapes help you learn better? Do you find yourself reading aloud or talking things out to gain a better understanding? If YES, you are probably an auditory learner.		• Where possible, develop mnemonic devices to assist in retention. • With visual material … develop your own audio explanation and description. • Engage with others online to discuss the material and your understanding.

(Continued)

Modality	Description	The degree to which this seems best for you (1 = yuk; 10 = perfecto)	Suggestion for maximizing
Kinesthetic learner (Tactile learner)	"Reach out and touch something!" Kinesthetic learners acquire information best when they can engage their tactile sense. They are at their best when the problem is hands-on ... a possible challenge when involved in online learning. Do you learn best when you can move about and handle things? Do you do well in classes in which there is a lab component? Do you learn better when you have an actual object in your hands rather than a picture of the object or a verbal or written description of it? In lecture situations, do you find yourself taking lots of notes, even doodling (while attending) or manipulating an object in your hands? If YES, you are probably a tactile/kinesthetic learner.		• When you can't actually touch the learning material, engage a squeeze ball as you read or listen. • Write notes, draw diagrams, even doodle as you listen or watch. • Connect material presented to real-life examples, applications, and case studies.

3.2: Environmental and Physical Factors

There are numerous approaches to defining and assessing learning styles. One developed by Rita Dunn (2000) expanded the view of learning style beyond a focus on sensory modalities to include other factors such as environment and physical elements. This model and the research it is founded upon shows that specific environmental and physical conditions can also influence one's ability to attend, process, and retain learning materials.

A little self-disclosure may help you to not only appreciate the power that environment and physical conditions can exert on your ability to process and retain information, but perhaps give you an opportunity to connect with your own personal experience. As a new undergraduate I made the personal commitment to really improve my study habits. I decided that after each class, when I had a break, I would go to the library and copy notes or prepare for the next class. Sounds good? Actually? Not so much.

The library at my university was a very beautiful, big, old, stone building with huge gathering areas, all with stone interiors, marble floors, and ceilings well over 20 feet high. The setting was extremely bright and warm and was furnished with large, long oak tables and chairs. Students were shushed (even after sneezing) and we all sat elbow to elbow at these long tables.

My experience in that setting was anything but conducive to processing information. I found that I felt edgy, had trouble sitting still, got up often for walks or drinks of water (and thus was shushed a lot), and generally found myself distracted by every little noise or movement. Fast forward 20 years when I was given the opportunity to assess my learning and performance style. Guess what? All the elements in this beautiful library were exactly the wrong ones for me. Oh, I eventually found that I could get more done more effectively by taking my work to the dimly lit, cool, informal, and noisy environment of the student center.

As you read on, perhaps you will discover something about your preferred learning and performance environments. You can use that knowledge to create the most conducive setting for success in your online course.

Environmental Factors

The environmental factors that appear to influence one's ability to concentrate and process information include noise, light, temperature, and even the formality of the setting. As you consider the environmental conditions in which you seem to not only be the most comfortable but are most able to focus and process information, ask yourself

- Do you prefer a noisy, busy setting?
- Do you need a well-lit setting to learn, study, or produce?
- Where are you on the desired temperature continuum? Warm? Cool?
- How about colors? Bright or subdued?
- Should your learning space be formal (e.g., desks and chairs) or informal (e.g., pillows)?

While each of these things may seem insignificant, the research is clear that these environmental factors can—when out of balance with your preferred style—result in physical discomfort, difficulty attending, and hindrance of processing and retaining information.

Physical Conditions

When considering the physiological domain, this model not only includes the sensory modalities of the VAKT model—processing information through visual, auditory, tactile or kinesthetic channels—but also your need for breaks to move about and the time of day during which you find yourself most energized, alert, and productive. Questions that you need to consider include the following:

- What is your VAKT?
- Do you "need" to snack while studying or learning?
- What is the optimal time for your concentration and productivity?
- Do you require freedom to move during learning?

3.3: And Your Style Is?

There are numerous assessment tools that you can access online (see the list in the additional resources section). You may find it very helpful to utilize one of these assessment tools (they are most often free). In the meantime, Table 3.1 describes these factors and invites you to identify the preferences (if any) that you may have. With a greater awareness of your preferred learning style, you will be able to structure your setting and your approach to online learning so that you maximize your ability to attend, process, and retain the materials presented.

Table 3.1. Setting the Stage for Learning

Domain	Element	Assessment (On a scale of 1–10 characterize your preference)	Example of programming to preference	Plan (How will you structure your learning setting to maximize these elements?)
Environment				
	Sound: Some people need quiet when they are learning, while others find that background noise, even music, serves to mask random sounds and helps them focus. Does "library" quiet make you uncomfortable? Easily distracted? Do you find that you readily block out television, radio, or random conversations when working?	White noise PLEASE (=10) Library SHUSH! (=1)	Sound: Soft nature sounds; music without lyrics; white noise machine. Quiet: Earphones to muffle noise.	

(Continued)

Domain	Element	Assessment (On a scale of 1–10 characterize your preference)	Example of programming to preference	Plan (How will you structure your learning setting to maximize these elements?)
	Light: Some people work best under very bright light; others need indirect or low lights. Do you feel a little more uncomfortable in a room with bright overhead lights? When at a desk do you use a bright, intense desk light? (Bright light preference?) When you are reading have others asked or suggested you turn on a light? (Low light preference?)	Bright and intense (=10) Not in the dark but subtle (=1)	Bright: No shades or window treatments; use full-spectrum light to simulate natural light. Low: Get a dimmer switch for lamps and overhead lighting.	
	Temperature: Cold and cool versus warm and hot. Under which temperature condition do you feel most alert and ready to "think" and work?	Not quite Nome, Alaska (=10) Heat lamp (without the tan) (=1)	Cold: Turn down the heat or turn up the A/C. Warm: Space heater or Granny's quilt.	

(Continued)

Domain	Element	Assessment (On a scale of 1–10 characterize your preference)	Example of programming to preference	Plan (How will you structure your learning setting to maximize these elements?)
Physical Conditions				
	Intake: Eat, drink, and be a learner! Do you find that you often have a cup of something to drink while you study or work at a desk? (intake) You find yourself chewing or nibbling on a snack while reading? (intake) Do you eat or drink only upon completion of a task? (no intake)	Snack fest (=10) Feed the mind, then the body (=1)	Intake: Easy, nutritious, non-messy snacks (think carrot sticks). No intake: Identify a treat to be enjoyed following the task at hand. Keep workspace clean and clear of food and drink.	
	Body Clock: Morning, evening, or in between? You are an early bird if you are up early even when you have a choice to sleep in. Do you find that you are generally the most productive in the morning? Or are you a night owl whose motor gets roaring when others are about to sleep?	Early bird (=10) Night owl (=1)	Early bird: Schedule your more difficult task for the morning hours (when possible). Night owl: Try to schedule tests in the afternoon or evening.	

(Continued)

Domain	Element	Assessment (On a scale of 1–10 characterize your preference)	Example of programming to preference	Plan (How will you structure your learning setting to maximize these elements?)
Mobility	Are you a person who can settle in and sit for long periods (low mobility) or do you find that you need to take frequent physical breaks and move about (high mobility)? Perhaps you are somewhere in between as a function of the level of interest in material?	A real settler (=10) Gots to get up (=1)	Low mobility: Set start and stop times to coincide with a complete unit or task. High mobility: Break up tasks into small sections; take a walk upon completion of each section or segment.	

SELF-REGULATION IN SERVICE OF ACADEMIC ACHIEVEMENT

Perhaps you were one of the people, like me, who found that, once you were living on your own, you really could eat chocolate cake for breakfast and nobody would suggest otherwise. As adults, you really have free rein to do whatever you want whenever you want. Perhaps that freedom has created minor problems for you.

Even though you have a lot of freedom, it is very likely that in most cases you moderate your behavior and maintain a responsible lifestyle. The explanation for such restraint is that you are showing what is termed self-regulation. Self-regulation skills are vital to our health, well-being, and especially to our academic success. However, self-regulation skills are not something we often think about or try to develop. To be successful in your online learning, the development and engagement of self-regulation skills will be essential.

4.1: Self-Regulation Skills and Online Learning

If there is one factor that appears significant for successful engagement with online education, it is the process of self-regulation. Think about it.

As an online student, you are expected to be self-initiating, self-directed, and employ the skills necessary to stay focused and achieve your learning outcomes. Such self-direction requires a conscious decision to make and manage time to engage in the learning tasks presented and to do so most efficiently and effectively. To be successful in such a self-directed approach to learning requires that you avoid distractions and rein in non-productive habits. Perhaps this seems obvious, but stepping up to the plate as a self-starter who is organized, motivated, and able to monitor and maintain progress is not always easy.

The challenge in being a self-disciplined and self-directed learner is that for most of our early school experience the elements necessary for academic progress were provided by others, including teachers, parents, even our peers. In our early years of developing self-regulation skills, our teachers and parents set and enforced rules, schedules, and tasks all designed to move us toward an educational goal. Eventually, you and I internalized these rules of behavior and conduct. We slowly became 'schoolized' and employed self-monitoring as a way of guiding our school behaviors and responses. But even with your years of self-regulation development, you may find that you are less than perfect at self-regulation. For example, have you found yourself procrastinating on a task to the point where you were pulling an "all-nighter"? Or perhaps there was a class you found challenging to even go to and, as a result, you may have chosen to cut class and hang out with friends.

Maybe you never experienced any of these failures in educational self-regulation. Still, there might have been an occasion when you simply didn't put the time into studying for a test or completing a project because something else in your life was more interesting. While all of these less-than-perfect examples of self-regulation are pretty normal, they certainly are times when you are not performing at your academic best, and it would be useful to understand how to either prevent these from occurring or how to intervene when they do.

Take a moment to review the questions for reflection that are posed in Exercise 4.1. It is helpful to realize your strengths and your challenges when it comes to educational self-regulation. Reviewing times of success and "failure" can help you identify contributors to your self-regulation and provide guidance as to what you can do to engage maximum self-regulation.

EXERCISE 4.1

Experience with Educational Self-Regulation

Directions: Assuming that you have experienced times of enjoyment and success in your academic pursuit, and times when it was a real struggle to deal with a particular assignment or course, it would be helpful to take a few moments to reflect on these experiences. Consider each of the following questions regarding your various experiences in school. Consider how you responded to these situations and how that response was effective (and thus should be retained) or less than effective (and thus should be adjusted for in the future).

Situation/experience	My response	Should I adjust? If so, how?
A course with a lot of reading assignments		
A course where the instructor was very liberal in assigning due dates for assignments		
A class that required group work (projects)		
A class that was completely or mostly lecture in nature		
An instructor who (as objectively as possible) was boring		
A required course, not something I would have chosen		
A class very early in the day		
A class at the end of a day		
A class in a large setting with numerous students		
A small class (for example, like a seminar)		
A class that required a class presentation		
A class that was discussion driven (required active student involvement)		

Difficulty with self-regulation translates into poor work habits, trouble concentrating, low motivation, and generally poor academic performance. A lack of self-regulation skills can result in a student failing to assign enough time to complete assignments; as a result, the student is often left turning in shoddy quality work or late assignments.

The good news is that self-regulation can be developed. You can strengthen the essential skills and habits that facilitate your ability to navigate your online learning experience successfully. So let's look at what you need to do.

4.2: The "What" of Self-Regulation and Learning

Several models describe the elements and actions that characterize self-regulation. One approach posits that self-regulated learners use metacognitive, motivational, and behavioral processes to achieve specific learning and performance goals (Zimmerman, 2011)

Metacognitive Processes

Metacognitive processes involve your thinking about your method of thinking. More specifically, it is the process you use to think about and evaluate the effectiveness of the strategies you use to complete a learning task. Metacognition refers to your awareness of what you do and do not know as you attempt to process the learning materials. Metacognition includes knowing when and where to use particular strategies for learning and problem solving, as well as how and why to use specific strategies. Your reflections on the cognitive strategies you use can result in your monitoring of these processes and their progress and then self-evaluating and adjusting strategies as needed.

Exercise 4.2 invites you to engage metacognition as you reflect on your approach to a recent learning task. When considering each of the questions posed, decide whether the approach you employed was successful or should be adjusted.

EXERCISE 4.2

My Metacognition

Directions: Consider each of the following questions as applied to your most recent learning activity. Decide if the approach you employed was successful or should be adjusted.

- Did I double check my understanding or my product?
- Did I make connections between what I was learning and what I had learned?
- Did I use some memory "tricks" like creating an image or a mnemonic to connect different concepts?
- Did I do a mini self-test to monitor my comprehension of a text?
- Did I review my work as a way of evaluating progress toward the completion of the task?
- Was I aware of distracting stimuli? If so, how did I respond? Did it work?

Attending to how your approach to processing information interacts with different assignments will help you understand the types of tasks that may be challenging and identify ways to be most effective with those tasks. For example, upon reflection you may discover that you get easily bored with reading lengthy, technical articles. With this awareness, you then can change your approach so that you break up the assigned readings into smaller units and take notes on each of these sections as a way of keeping you focused and engaged.

Motivational Processes

Motivational processes are those that you employ to get your motor running. It is the various techniques that help get you started on a task, sustain your focus on the tasks, engage goal-directed activities, AND ignore distractions.

Chapter 5 goes into greater detail on the elements of motivation and how to use these to maximize your academic achievement. Still, one of the factors to motivation that deserves special attention is the act of goal setting. Chapter 6 provides a discussion on the topic and process of goal setting as a valuable element to your online success.

Behavioral Processes

Self-regulatory behavioral processes include "positive" behaviors that are typically associated with successful task completion (Zimmerman, 2011). As applied to online learning, the actions that need to be employed include (a) matching your learning style preference to your approach to task completion (see Chapter 3); (b) applying time and task management strategies (see Chapter 7), and (c) engaging motivational strategies that help you keep your eye on the prize (i.e., avoid temptations and distractions) (see Chapter 5).

These processes appear to take center stage at different points along the continuum of planning, doing, and evaluating your work on a task, unit, or course.

Planning

If you don't know where you are going, it is likely that you won't get there. So as you approach an online course or assignment, it is essential to develop a plan of attack. This process starts with surveying what is required and being sure that you understand the task at hand. If not … ASK!

It is also vital to think about your expectations about the upcoming experience and the interest or value you place on engaging in the experience. It is important to find value in the process or the experience itself or be able to remind yourself of the importance that you are placing on achieving the outcome of this particular activity. What is the "payoff" for being successful with this task, this assignment, this unit … this course? Identifying what you hope to gain, even before you start the educational experience, will help you remain motivated.

Another thing you will need to do during this planning stage is review what will be required of you and outline the strategies you will employ to get it all done. Once the course or unit has started, you need to select a plan to do the actual work. This is an excellent time to review your specific learning style (remember Chapter 3?) and identify the conditions and approaches that have worked for you in the past. For example, will you take notes while viewing videos? Do you need to hear the material and maybe use recorded self-explaining concepts after reading? In addition to identifying the strategies you will employ, you need to structure a schedule or a timeline to guide your efforts. Having a schedule not only helps to keep you focused but also can be motivational and rewarding as you see milestones being accomplished (see Chapter 7).

Monitoring

I'm not sure if you ever ran a marathon or mini-marathon; if not, perhaps you have watched one. Ever notice that many of the runners at the starting line start their watches? Are they really that concerned about what time it is?

As I am sure you are aware, the purpose of the watch setting is to help them keep pace. Those who are competitive runners know their current level of performance and the speed which will optimally bring them to their goal. They don't want to fall behind—nor do they want to exceed their optimal pace. The watch provides them with the data they need to modify their pace to keep on track as planned.

Monitoring the degree to which you are engaging with your strategies for learning and the apparent achievement that is occurring is an essential self-regulating behavior. In the monitoring phase, you will review the strategies you are employing, measuring the outcomes against your expectations, and then making real-time adjustments to your plans as needed. During the process, you need to do a critical and honest self-evaluation. Exercise 4.3 invites you to reflect on your current or most recent online experience. Remember, if any of your answers is a "no," then it is time to adjust!

EXERCISE 4.3

An Invitation to Monitor

Directions: It is important to assess not only the degree to which you achieved your ultimate goals but also to monitor your progress toward those goals. Using your current or most recent online experience, ask yourself the following. If the answers are no, consider ways to adjust your approach and strategies to get you back on the path toward academic success.

- Am I concentrating on learning the material?
- Do I understand all the critical points of the material?
- Are the study strategies I'm using helping me learn the training material?
- Am I setting goals to help me remember the material after I finish the course?
- Would I do better on the next quiz if I studied more?
- Am I setting goals to ensure I have a thorough understanding of the training material?
- Do I know enough about the material to answer the questions correctly on the next assessment for this module?
- Am I enjoying the process?
- Am I progressing toward my goals?

Reflection

Okay, so the task is complete or the course is over. What should you do? Celebrate? Absolutely!

It is important to reward yourself to celebrate the completion of an assignment or the end of a course. Once the celebration is over, you need to reflect upon your experience to critically assess how you did in terms of your initial planning, the strategies you chose and implemented, and the degree to which the process and the outcomes were as desired. In this reflection phase, you should attempt to synthesize everything you learned about yourself as a student and your approach to learning, identifying the good, the bad, and dare I say the ugly. This reflection will help you determine what works and what should be altered or replaced. Exercise 4.4 provides you the opportunity to reflect on your most recent online experience and gather the data that will guide your adjustments when engaging with the next task or course.

EXERCISE 4.4

Reflecting and Adjusting

Directions: Below you will find a table that presents questions for reflections and invites you to not only reflect on your experience but develop recommendations or suggestions on how you will adjust your approach to the next online task or course.

Questions to consider	Steps to take to improve the next time
Were you satisfied with the experience and outcome? If not, why?	
Are you happy with the effort invested? If not, what held you back?	
Which strategies did you employ that helped to keep you on task, on schedule, and motivated?	
What strategies did you employ that were in service of your learning style preferences? Did you experience anything that ran contrary to your learning style preferences which you need to adjust in the future?	
Reflecting on this experience—assume that you were turning back the clock and starting over, what would you do differently? (let this guide your plan for your next experience)	

4.3: Persistence—A Key to Success

Persistence is perhaps the biggest key to success in online learning. Students who succeed are those who are willing to tolerate technical problems, able to push through minor frustrations, seek help when needed, work daily on every class, and persist through challenges. Students who can persist in the face of frustrations and barriers are those who engage effort regulation.

Effort regulation or effort management refers to the ability to take control over your attention and focus even in situations that present as distractions. Effort regulation is reflected in your ability to succeed even when you are dealing with a difficult task or experiencing barriers to your performance (think tech issues). Self-regulated learners tend to keep their efforts and attention when they face less-than-exciting tasks and numerous distractions. Effort regulation reflects learners' determination to achieve their targets, and it also affects their use of learning strategies. Therefore, effort regulation is substantially influential in academic achievement. Exercise 4.5 invites you to reflect on your ability to achieve even when the task is less than exciting or when things keep popping up to interfere with your achievement. Recognizing how you have successfully persisted in less-than-optimal situations will not only remind you that you can do it but will also highlight how you did this.

EXERCISE 4.5

Effort Regulation

Directions: While it would be ideal if every course you experienced and every task that you attempted went smoothly and resulted in the achievement of the outcome you desired, such is not typically the case. Identify a course or assignment that (a) you found to be less than exciting or (b) presented several barriers to your performance.

Now describe the elements that, while they should have been problematic, you were able to push through and become successful. Remembering how you succeeded in these less-than-desirable conditions will reinforce your belief in yourself as well as highlight the strategies you employed to be successful.

Effort management is essential to academic success because it not only signifies goal commitment but also regulates the continued use of learning strategies. Effort management is the cure to academic procrastination.

Table 4.1. Attacking Academic Procrastination

Set small task/goals Large tasks can often seem overwhelming. It is beneficial to be realistic about the amount of time/energy you are willing (able?) to expend at any one time and use that as the framework for setting an achievable goal. Just getting moving and taking the first step—especially when that step is not exhausting—will chip away at your academic procrastination and create momentum.
Get up! Start doing! When procrastinating, we often spend more time thinking about what we are supposed to be doing than doing it. This thinking—unless we are strategizing on how to attack the task—is not only a waste of time, it can make the task seem overwhelming. Sitting there waiting to get motivated typically doesn't work. Get moving, and the motivation will follow. Again, keep the cost low. Tell yourself, "I will take 10 minutes and do (identify one specific thing)." Small? Yes. But doing one thing is better than nothing. Move—pick up the book, open the online site, contact your professor. Do SOMETHING!
Organize in a way that reflects your learning style You know your best time of day for performing, so plan a small task to accomplish during that time. Keep it small … keep it brief, but keep it going. Arrange your work area so that it is comfortable and inviting. Remove distractions.
Reward yourself Set up your tasks in such a way that you can reward yourself upon completion. If you are having a difficult time getting started, try to set up something that you love doing (maybe a video game, watching a television show, working out, etc.) to be earned by performing a small learning task. For example, make a "deal" with yourself that you will only log on to your game site after completing some small section of the assignment. Rewarding your achievements, especially those that have been less than totally enjoyable, is a good practice. For some, it may be enjoying a dessert or watching a favorite show or playing a computer game. Whatever your pleasure, engage that activity as soon after the completion of your academic work as possible and consciously remind yourself that this is a reward for a job well done.
Take time out Taking time out or time off may seem counterintuitive, but intentionally setting aside time to allow yourself to be "less than productive" can increase your chances of staying focused when you need to. Having a break in your planned schedule will help you feel less trapped when you engage with your work and thus make it more appealing to start.

If you ever engaged in academic procrastination, you know that it can adversely affect your academic progress and achievement. The lower levels of goal commitment and the smaller amount of time and energy invested are all characteristics of academic procrastination and are antithetical to academic success. Given the freedom and flexibility that is offered by most online courses, along with a shift of responsibility to you as a self-directed learner, procrastination can be a significant problem.

For some people, maybe you, the idea of waiting until the last minute is just the element of pressure they need to get their motor running. If that is your most effective style, it is wise to continue. However, given the stress that such a process places upon you, you may want to "experiment" with some of the techniques described later that will result in less procrastination. Table 4.1 provides several simple steps to attack academic procrastination and get on with getting on.

MOTIVATION

C hapter 4 highlighted the need to engage in self-regulation to be successful in your online courses. In addition to self-regulation, your success will depend upon your ability to be motivated to actually employ these self-regulated behaviors. To be successful, you need to tap your intrinsic and extrinsic motivation to energize you for all that you will be required to accomplish (Matuga, 2009).

The idea of motivation is certainly not new to you. What might be surprising is that you are always motivated. I know that probably doesn't seem to ring true, especially when you think of it in terms of attacking your schoolwork.

However, as a human, you are always moved to do something. When it comes to a particular area of your life, you may declare that you are NOT motivated. That would be true if you refer to doing a specific task. However, while you may not be motivated to work on the research paper, you are motivated to do something. Sleep? Play? Exercise?

As you can imagine, academic motivation and engagement are vital pieces of your academic performance. If unmotivated (academically), you may find yourself disengaged in your class and struggling to keep the focus necessary to understand and process the information provided. Without the proper level of motivation you may find that you begin to fall behind and—with a mounting stack of tasks to complete—your motivation to avoid, rather than engage, may be driving your decisions.

Understanding the elements that contribute to your motivation will help you manipulate those elements in such a way as to call forth the academic motivation you need to succeed.

5.1: Motivation—Its Elements

Take a brief moment to identify times when you were motivated—truly pushed—toward engaging in some activity or achieving some goal or outcome. This doesn't have to be in terms of your schooling. It could be around some activity like exercising, some type of competition in which you were engaged, or even a desire to learn a new tune on a musical instrument.

Without knowing the specifics of your experience, I think I can guess that a couple of elements were involved. First, I bet you found the actual activity or its outcome to be attractive or desirable. Second, it is most likely that, before actually engaging in the motivated activity, you had a good sense and a firm belief that this activity was something that you could do successfully.

Am I right?

If so, I wish I could take the credit—but that credit needs to go the value-expectancy theory of motivation. While we do not need to get overly technical, this theory provides a simple way to not only understand what conditions and circumstances will elicit our motivation to engage, but gives us direction as to how to manipulate these conditions and these elements to increase our motivation when desired.

5.2: Factors Contributing to Motivational Level

The value-expectancy theory posits that the effort a person is willing to expend on a task is a product of two factors interacting with each other. The first factor is the degree to which one values the anticipated outcome or payoff if successful. The second element refers to the degree to which a person expects or believes that they can perform the task successfully and thus achieve the desired outcome. The theory places these two elements into the following formula: *Motivation = Value × Expectancy*. A point that should be highlighted is that this formula is multiplicative and not summative. In other words, if one element is low, motivation will be low. If one of the elements is zero or absent, as would be the case where you see no value or hold no expectation of success, then your motivation to engage will be zero.

Let's do a little mind experiment. How would you like it if I promised to give you $1,000,000?

There is a chance I may have awakened your interest. If so, then we have part one of the equation, value—more technically subjective value (i.e., the value that you are placing on the outcome). Assuming that you are not flooded with money, the million dollar payoff would hold high subjective value.

But just as you are thinking of all that you could do with that money (i.e., value), you probably are starting to wonder or even question what it is that you have to do to acquire that payoff? Okay. Fair question.

So, here is the deal. In order for you to get my one million dollars all you have to do is leap over the Statue of Liberty without the aid of any artificial device. Hmmm.

Somehow, I don't see you rushing out the door, sneakers on, eagerly getting to the Statue of Liberty to do your leap. Why? Because even though you may highly value the offer, your expectation of being able to succeed at the task is zero. When applied to the formula, High value × (times) zero expectation of success = zero motivation.

We can reverse the elements and still end up with low to zero motivation. Here is a ridiculous example. If I asked you to write out the alphabet 100 times and then promised that I would give you a dollar if you were successful, there is a good chance that, other than thinking something was wrong with me, you would simply ignore the offer. Why? High expectation of success (you can write the alphabet) times zero subjective value (Really? One dollar?) equals zero motivation.

I think you get the idea. The benefit of understanding this formula and approach to the concept of motivation is that it can help you engage your motivation by engaging these two factors. Learning how to increase the subjective value of an academic task while at the same time arranging that task in such a way as to increase your expectations of success will go a long way to increasing your motivation and your chance for academic success. If value and expectancy go up, so will your motivation to engage with the task.

5.3: Task Values

When attempting to identify the value of any task, we should try answering the questions, "Do I really want to do this?" and "Why?"

In answering these questions, we may realize that there is just something about doing the task and actually engaging in the process or the activity that is, in and of itself, enjoyable and satisfying. We may also discover that there are other tasks that we value, not because we enjoy the process or the experience, but because they provide an outcome that we want to have. So these tasks have very little intrinsic value but gain value as a means to some desired end. The bigger the payoff, the more the task or activity is valued.

Intrinsic Motivation

There are some things you are motivated to do simply because you find satisfaction in doing that particular activity or task. In these situations where the activity—the process itself—is its own payoff, we have intrinsic motivation.

Take a moment to think about those activities which generally have little or small payoffs but seem to give you a sense of joy or satisfaction simply by doing them. Perhaps you enjoy playing an instrument, even though you are not performing for money or applause—the joy you feel is an intrinsic motivation. Similarly, if you find cooking to be an enjoyable activity regardless of the meal produced, then you know the experience of intrinsic motivation. There are times when being involved in your schoolwork can be something that in itself is satisfying (i.e., intrinsically motivating). When you were engaged in these types of intrinsically satisfying activities, you probably found that you were not only involved in the activity but almost consumed by it. There are times when you are in the flow—perhaps losing awareness of the time spent or even the presence of others. These are times of very high intrinsic value.

Extrinsic Motivation

Now it would be wonderful if everything you did, especially in terms of your schoolwork, could be intrinsically satisfying. However, that is not always the case for school, work, or life in general.

When you are moved or motivated not so much by the joy of the activity but the hope of achieving some outcome, your engagement in service of acquiring this desired end is said to be extrinsically motivated. In situations of extrinsic motivation, the activity or behavior itself is not the goal or the reason for enactment but is merely the means to acquiring a desired end.

Perhaps you are a person who truly loves to work out. You find the process and the actual physical experience to be its own reward. For you exercise elicits intrinsic motivations. But if you are someone who is not thrilled with physical exertion but you truly have a desire to lose weight, then going to the gym or working out is a means to that end. The "end" of losing weight is what is valued. This is an example of extrinsic motivation.

In most common terms, extrinsic motivation typically directs us to that which is seen as a reward or payoff. In brick-and-mortar classrooms, students will often work for a grade or an honor or even teacher praise. These are all examples of extrinsic motivators.

There are many good reasons to work hard in school. You might want a greater level of personal satisfaction with your future career. Or perhaps it's personal pride in your accomplishments. Or maybe you are seeking the wider range of opportunities available to you with higher education or a higher income.

Payoffs can be immediate—like when you feel good about being able to answer the question in class—they can be a little more remote (that is coming somewhere in the future)—such as when better grades help you get into grad school or a desirable job.

For now, it doesn't matter if your payoffs are immediate or remote as long as they are real ... and personal (YOURS).

5.4: I Think I Can ... I Think I Can!

The second part of our motivation equation (remember?) is that in addition to seeing value in the task or activity we are asked to engage, we must also believe that there is a very high probability that we can succeed at the task. The concept of self-efficacy refers to a person's level of belief about their capabilities to produce designated levels of performance that exercise influence over events that affect their lives (Bandura, 2005). Self-efficacy is specific to the task being attempted. High self-efficacy in one area may not coincide with high self-efficacy in another. Just as high confidence in playing the viola may not be matched with high confidence in playing basketball, high self-efficacy in one science course does not necessarily accompany high self-efficacy when enrolling in a literature course. But elements contributing to self-efficacy can be manipulated to increase the presence of this value element for your motivation.

Believing you can be successful is key to your level of motivation when approaching a task. If your belief in your ability to achieve the desired outcome is low or nonexistent, then your motivation to engage will be low or even nonexistent (think about the million-dollar challenge to leap the Statue of Liberty).

Research has consistently demonstrated that students who exhibit high self-efficacy work harder, persist longer, persevere in the face of adversity, have greater optimism and lower anxiety, and as a result are more successful in their academic pursuits than are those with low self-efficacy. The more self-efficacious a student's beliefs are, the more they will engage in setting realistic yet challenging goals, monitoring their performance, adjusting as needed, and producing higher academic achievement (Zimmerman, 2000)

Now we need to state a caveat. Belief in your abilities will work only as long as that belief gives form to your success. Success or mastery of tasks requires not only the belief and expectation of success (that serves as an element of motivation) but also employing the knowledge and skill necessary to perform in the task. There is little value in personal self-efficacy if it is based on delusion. While such a belief without substance may initially spur an individual into action, the absence of knowledge and skill necessary for success will quickly place the person in failure. This failure will work to undermine their self-efficacy when considering future, similar tasks. It is important, therefore, that you structure your tasks—setting meaningful and achievable goals in a way that not only encourages belief in your ability to be successful but will result in evidence of that success.

Given the value of high self-efficacy, what can you do to increase your belief and your expectation of success? One source contributing to your level of self-efficacy is your own previous experience with success. Given this fact, it is important when approaching a new assignment or task to

a. <u>Set Functional Goals.</u> Functional goals are those that are specific, concrete, and measurable. Most importantly, functional goals are those which are achievable WITH effort. Chapter 6 discusses goal setting in more detail.

b. <u>Monitor Progress.</u> It is important to develop a method for assessing your progress. Often the "payoff" of your efforts rests in the final outcome. It is important to provide "payoffs" all along the way. One way to do this is to set markers or goal posts for each task, each assignment, and each online encounter, and check them off once accomplished. It may sound simple, but it is effective.

c. <u>Reward Yourself.</u> Reward yourself after reaching or exceeding each of the markers that you set in the previous step. The reward may be as simple as giving yourself a pat on the back, a word of praise, or a dramatic crossing off of the marker. It is also useful to provide yourself with a tangible payoff. Save your snack or treat or, if of age, libation for after successful completion of the task or the designated section of that task. Finally, upon completing a significant project or unit or even the course, brag to your friends. It really is an achievement, and you have a right to crow.

d. <u>Effort Counts.</u> There are situations in which an immediate outcome is hard to identify and thus hard to reward. Think in terms of a hard workout. Evidence of increased tone or muscle mass or even stamina is most likely not immediate. But you know the effort you put into the work. You know whether you slacked off or really pushed it. It is beneficial to the maintenance of your motivation and the development of self-efficacy to reward yourself for the effort. The same is true when engaged in an online task. Sometimes goal achievement may be delayed, but the work you are doing to move toward the goal should be rewarded.

5.5: What Motivates Me?

To be successful, an online student has to want to succeed. This want, this motivation will exist when the student values the anticipated outcome of the online course or program (extrinsic motivation) and can find joy and satisfaction in the very process of engaging in the tasks assigned (intrinsic motivation).

It would be helpful, as you attempt to motivate yourself for an online experience, to reflect upon and reaffirm the goals that you seek as a result of taking this course or engaging this program. Exercise 5.1 invites you to take a moment to identify concrete outcomes that you hope to achieve as a result of taking an online course. Taking a moment to identify these payoffs and reminding yourself of these as you progress through a course will help you to maintain your motivation, especially at times when the activity or task itself is less than enjoyable. If you post these where you can see them daily, they will help keep the fire and desire burning!

EXERCISE 5.1

Engaging My Extrinsic Motivation

Directions: This exercise can and should be applied to your engagement in a specific learning assignment or task as well as in reference to your enrollment in a particular course or the overall online program.

Step 1: With a piece of paper, brainstorm as many possible outcomes as you can imagine following the successful completion of *(insert task, course, program, etc.)*. As you may know, the goal here during the brain-storming stage is to generate as many responses as possible without evaluating feasibility or even desirability.

Step 2: Review your list of outcomes. Choose the three that not only reflect those which you personally value but reflect those that excite you.

Step 3: POST those payoffs, those outcomes … those goals that you have identified as valuable. Get creative with your postings. Place reminders at your work station. Post a note on your text or material. Keep this evidence of the payoff in your FACE.

In addition to engaging your extrinsic motivation, it is helpful to engage intrinsic motivation. Exercise 5.2 invites you to consider some of the activities (academic and non-academic) that you do solely for their intrinsic value. These are tasks or activities that may result in some outcome, but achieving that outcome is less important than the experience of doing the task. For some, this may be something like reading a novel, going to a movie, or meeting friends for coffee. Getting to the end or gaining some incredible insight may not be what motivates engaging in these activities. It is merely engaging in the activity that is the payoff.

As you review the exercise, you will see that it not only asks you to identify such tasks or activities but, when possible, to identify specific characteristics of these tasks and these activities that contribute to your intrinsic motivation. The idea is for you to identify these elements and, as much as possible, incorporate them into your online experiences.

EXERCISE 5.2

Activities with Intrinsic Value

Directions: This exercise has two parts. Part 1, simply brainstorm things that you like to do in an ongoing or recurrent way. Just list the activity (e.g., shop, swim, eat, do chemistry experiments, write programs) in Column A. Part 2 will take a little more reflection and introspection. In Column B, write down as concretely and as accurately as you can what it is about this activity that you find of value. Getting in touch with those things that are intrinsically satisfying could be useful in your approach to specific learning tasks.

Column A: Activities I enjoy and value (Include academic and non-academic activities)	Column B: What is it about this activity that makes it so valued by me?	Implication for online course strategies
Academic		
(example): small group projects	1. I like the sense of connecting, camaraderie. 2. I enjoy taking the lead—providing leadership. 3. I believe more heads are better than one.	1. try to connect with my peers, even when the task is not a group work task; invite them to share feedback on my work 2. reach out and connect to see if I could develop an online study group 3. when connecting with peers is not possible, I will share what I am doing with family and friends and get their ideas and feedback
Non-Academic		
(example): working out	1. I like pushing myself to get to a new goal. 2. I love the feeling—the physical feeling. 3. I enjoy the people at the gym—I work out with friends.	1. need to set specific goals 2. might have to move around—do some quick aerobics as a way of breaking up periods of sitting 3. try to connect with others online—socially and academically

GOAL SETTING
AN EYE ON THE PRIZE

Y ogi Berra, the New York Yankees baseball team's Hall of Fame catcher who was known for his humorous yet poignant comments observed, *"If you don't know where you are going, you'll end up someplace else."* This is true for all aspects of life, and it definitely applies to taking an online course.

6.1: Why Goals?

You are not new to goal setting. Perhaps you have experienced a competitive goal, such as winning at a sporting event; a personal growth goal, such as learning to play the guitar; or something like identifying a place to go on spring break.

Given your own experience with goals and goal setting, you probably can appreciate that taking on a project or beginning some adventure without a goal—without a sense of why and what you hope to achieve—can result in a lot of wasted energy and misdirection. It is difficult to act without a clear picture of where you are going or intend to go. This is true for your education and your online course engagement.

6.2: Goals: Mapping Direction and Progress

Knowing what you desire—what you hope to attain—will not only help you begin to plan how to get from here to there but will also provide you a means for monitoring your progress. For example, imagine that you were thinking about escaping during spring break. Would you have to decide what it was you were seeking? Scenery? Friends? A specific type of weather, setting, or activity?

Now you may not sit down and think about these specifics, but they are the goals that direct your selection of a destination. With the destination as your reference point, you begin to plan out the strategies to get there. Will you drive? Fly? Walk? (Okay, I probably pushed it too far.)

In this little example, you can see that knowing what you desire (your goal) sets the stage for developing your plan of attack, and it will allow you to monitor your progress. You know the routine. Flying? In this case, you monitor your progress getting to the airport, parking, grabbing a shuttle, going through TSA checkpoints, and whew ... making the flight. If you are driving, there is always the "Oh, look, we are entering such and such state," that lets us know we are going in the right direction and making progress.

Clear, concrete, and achievable goals can help you focus and gain a sense of purpose, both of which can serve to motivate you to continue to exert the time and energy needed for advancement. When you know where you wish to go and what you need to do to get there, you will be able to focus and mobilize yourself for action. This is true for many aspects of your life ... including your academic pursuits.

6.3: Challenges to Goal Setting

While goal setting is a critical element of your successful online educational experience, it can come with some unique challenges. One of the challenges that you may encounter in trying to set your goal(s) is that you may undermine your goal setting with thoughts like "I can't do that," or "I don't have the resources," or "There is too much going on in my life."

No Constraints—Expanding Your Goals

The conditions of your life at this point may make achieving your initial goal highly unlikely. But even with that as a point for consideration, it is beneficial to take all of these concerns, real or imagined, out of the equation as you make your first stab at identifying your goals. While your initial "wish list" will need to be reshaped in a way that reflects reality and takes shape as SMART goals, your initial thoughts about the outcome you desire should not be so constrained.

One strategy that can be used to free you up to identify your goals is to respond to the "Miracle Question" (Berg & Miller, 1992). While the term "miracle" may lead you to conclude that the question is designed to encourage you to place your faith in the occurrence of magic or miracles, this is not the case. The miracle question is simply a future-oriented question that invites you to envision a future time when you and your world (or, in this case, your educational experience) were precisely as you wished it to be.

The use of a 'miracle' focus helps you access your creative capacities that are most adaptive when not constricted by the realities of life. The miracle question invites you to think about goals in ways that do not trigger thoughts that nullify the hope and belief in the possibility of achieving those goals. It is a process that invites you to think out of the box. Exercise 6.1 invites you to respond to the miracle question as a way of gaining an expanded view of what you hope to achieve with the successful completion of this online course.

EXERCISE 6.1

Miracle Question

Directions: Read the following question and begin to list all the ways you think to respond. You may want to reread the question a couple of times to see if other thoughts come to mind.

Suppose that while you are sleeping tonight, a miracle happens. The miracle is that everything you hoped to accomplish and achieve in this one course happened. However, because you are sleeping, you don't know that the miracle has happened. So when you wake up tomorrow morning, what will be different that will tell you that a miracle has happened? What will you notice that is different? What, if anything, will others notice that is different?

_____

_____

_____

_____

_____

_____

Is It a Goal ... or a Means to a Goal?

It is not unusual for a person to establish a goal only to find that it was not really a goal but a means to the real goal. Think about the person whose goal in life is to "retire." Is that the goal, or is retiring just one way they can free themselves up to do other activities?

Perhaps you feel that this distinction is not that important. What's the difference if retirement is the goal or a means to the goal? Well, the value in understanding this and learning to push yourself to identify the underlying goals that you are seeking is that there is one goal, but there are many pathways. So if the goal was actually to be in a state of "retirement," then having to prolong one's work life would be a grand disappointment. However, if retirement was just a condition, a means that would allow the person to achieve their underlying goal of pursuing hobbies, for example, then maybe there is a creative way that those hobbies could be pursued (even in modified versions) during the extended period of employment. Knowing the bottom-line goal will allow us to be creative in identifying the various ways this goal could be achieved thus giving us options if one path gets blocked.

So perhaps your goal for this course is an A. Ask yourself, "Is that really the goal?"

It might be.

Getting an A in this or any other course can be the terminal point, the final outcome desired. It can be the actual goal you are shooting for with nothing else in mind. Sometimes, however, getting an A in this course may be but one step to achieving the actual desired goal, which might be to make the dean's list.

So if gaining an A was the goal, and you fell short of the grade, then you would be disappointed and unsatisfied. However, if your goal was to make the dean's list and you got a B in this one course, you would know that there are other avenues to acquire the desired outcome. You may realize that achieving the dean's list is still possible if you can get an A in your second course. In this case, even though you may be disappointed in not getting the A, you remain motivated on your path to your actual goal.

Before we discuss the development of effective goals, take a moment to identify just one goal that you have for engaging with an online course. In Part 1 of Exercise 6.2, you are invited to write out this goal. As you can see, Exercise 6.2 is multipart, and we will return to it as we progress through this chapter.

EXERCISE 6.2

Developing My Goal

Directions: The current exercise is a multi-part exercise that invites you to create a meaningful and useful goal. You will be asked to return to various sections of this exercise as you move through this chapter.

Part 1: Goal
In the space below, describe what it is that you hope to achieve by taking this online course. While you may have many goals, select just one.

Example: I want to do well in this course.

_____

_____

_____

_____

_____

Part 2: Specificity

Review the goal you described in Part 1 and answer the following questions. How would it look if you achieved this goal? What would be different, something that others may notice? Can you rephrase the goal so that it is in precise terms?

Example: I will get an A in this course.

_____

_____

_____

_____

_____

Part 3: Measurable

Is your goal measurable? Can you translate the goal in a way that you can observe when it is achieved? What data or assessment would you use?

Example: My goal is to make a grade of A, as recorded on my transcript.

_____

_____

_____

_____

_____

Part 4: Achievable

Review your goal and include elements that will indicate that your goal is both achievable and that you have a plan in mind for achieving it. It helps to make your goal something that you need to stretch for while at the same time realistic.

Example: While this is my first online course and I have to be more self-disciplined, using the strategies I've used in previous classes to earn an A—recopying my notes, following each online lecture, and organizing them into study sheets—will help me achieve an A in this course.

_____

_____

_____

_____

_____

Part 5: Results

Take time to brainstorm all the positive results (payoffs) that will occur as a result of reaching your goal in this course. The more, the better. You may want to post these, as they can contribute to your level of motivation.

Example: If I attain an A for this course, it will
- position me to get the internship placement I would like,
- place me on the dean's list,
- help me get accepted into the master's program to which I applied,
- be a personal point of pride,
- help me believe I can do this,
- allow me to tease my brother since my GPA will be higher than his, and
- help me keep my student loan.

Part 6: Timely
Identify the timeline for achieving your goal.

Example: I will recopy my notes immediately following each lecture, expanding them to include study notes. I will also record my grades each week as a way to monitor that my average grade is at least a 93% (an A).

Once you are clear about your goal, it is essential to make sure it is a SMART goal.

6.4: Setting SMART Goals

If your goals are impersonal, vague, overly generalized, or unrealistic, you may find that they are not only valueless but may increase your sense of frustration and hopelessness. Such unrealistic or ill-conceived goals will undermine your motivation.

For goals to be useful, they should be SMART. Goals that will serve you well are **S**pecific, **M**easurable, **A**ttainable, **R**esult-focused, and **T**imely.

Specificity

Specific goals have been found to produce higher levels of performance and success than ambiguous goals. Let's assume your goals for this class are to (1) do well and (2) feel smart. What exactly would it look like if you reach these goals? How might others know you have achieved your goals?

For these goals to be useful, they need to be more specific, more concrete, more observable. What does "doing well" look like? Is it a particular grade? Is it gaining some comments from your instructor or your peers? How about "feeling smart"? Is that an actual physical feeling? Is it an emotional state? Or is it a sense of self-efficacy, believing that you have the skills and knowledge necessary to succeed at school? If we can't put our finger on our goals, how will we know when we achieve them?

Having goals that are specific will make it easier to tailor strategies to achieve the goal. For example, if the purpose of "doing well" is redefined as getting an A on this test, you will understand that you have to commit time and energy to studying the materials covered on the upcoming test. Similarly, if "feeling good" actually translates into gaining feedback from the instructor, then you might understand that one path to that goal is to participate and invite feedback by asking questions and offering answers.

You are invited to return to Exercise 6.2, Part 2, to practice making your goals specific.

Measurable

It is important to frame your goals in ways that allow you to measure progress, because, as noted, seeing progress is motivating. Some goals lend themselves to being measured in that they are easily quantified. So if your goal was to spend 30 minutes studying, you could set a timer as a means of announcing that you have reached your goal. If the goal is to get a 90% or more on the test, the grade received will demonstrate whether or not you attained your goal. Sometimes, however, your goal may be a reflection of some subjective feeling or internal state, like feeling proud of the work you've accomplished. This type of goal doesn't lend itself to observation and direct measurement. However, one strategy that can be used to measure and monitor your goal achievement is to develop a subjective scale of goal achievement.

If, for example, you were using a sense of pride as your goal, it would help to identify a specific event or time when you felt very proud of your performance. Draw a horizontal line and place a brief description (as a reminder) of that event at the extreme right end. The short description will help you remember the time and the feeling. You could even assign a number to that experience—let's say 10 (out of 10).

Now, identify a time in your life or an experience when your sense of pride in what you produced was low, a time when you really were not happy with the final product nor your effort. Place that description on the left end of the line and label it 1. With these two subjective markers as your reference point you can evaluate your current state of pride in your work and place it on this continuum. Revisiting your internal sense of pride will help you monitor progress across the scale to 10 (and beyond). It would be helpful for you to return to Exercise 6.2, this time Part 3, and check to see whether your goal is measurable.

Attainability

Attainability is another critical characteristic of effective goals. To be effective, goals need to realistically attainable or achievable given your resources, capabilities, and other demands that you may be experiencing. Perhaps you desire an A on an assignment. You need to assess the feasibility of that given, for example, that you had to take on a new job that is extremely challenging, your grandparents have just moved into your house, and you are presently fighting the flu. Given these conditions, the A may simply be beyond your reach (at least for this assignment).

Goals need to be reasonably challenging and require you to stretch yourself, but they also need to be realistic and achievable. When goals are too challenging or unrealistic, it is quite possible you will become extremely frustrated and may even begin to believe it hopeless. This would undermine your motivation since, as you remember from Chapter 5, motivation is a function of value multiplied by expectancy!

In Exercise 6.2, Part 4, you are asked to review your initial goal to see if it is achievable. It is important to take a moment to consider all of the things going on in your life and, if need be, change your goal from the "wished for" to the feasible.

Result-Focused

When we discussed the idea of motivation (Chapter 5), we noted the importance of finding value in what you were doing or what you were achieving. It is important to consider the impact or result of achieving your goal. How will making this goal impact you and your life? What precisely is the payoff you will receive? Are there intrinsic as well as extrinsic payoffs for achieving your goal(s)?

It is helpful to place a reminder of the value—the payoff—for achieving these goals since such a reminder can be a stimulus for ongoing motivation.

In Part 5 of Exercise 6.2 you are asked to brainstorm all of the payoffs that will result from achieving your goal. It is essential to identify as many of these payoffs as possible since they will contribute to your level of motivation.

Time

The final characteristic of an effective goal is that it is time-bound—that is, it has an identified target date/time. Timelines not only serve as motivators but also provide you with a means for gauging progress and adjusting strategies if need be (see Chapter 7).

The timeline needs to be reasonable and flexible, thus allowing for adjustment as progress occurs. The idea is for the timeline to serve as a support for goal achievement, not contribute to your stress. If the timetable needs to be modified given unexpected events or circumstances, adjust it. It is your goal, and you can change it.

6.5: Just Do It!

Exercise 6.3 invites you to return to the wish list of goals that you established in Exercise 6.1, pick those that are a priority, and develop them as SMART goals. Given the value of SMART goals as contributors to your motivation and ability to monitor progress and assess the effectiveness of strategies, it is suggested that you post these in a place that will be visible as you engage with your course. It is also valuable to monitor your success and review the steps that contributed to that success (see Exercise 6.4)

EXERCISE 6.3

My Goals

Directions: Review the various outcomes, or goals, that you generated when engaging with the "miracle question" (Exercise 6.1). Identify those that are genuinely priorities for you as you approach your online course (or, if you prefer, as you approach a specific online assignment). Rewrite these goals as SMART goals. Print them out and keep them visible in your study area to encourage your motivation.

Example: I will recopy my lecture notes, form these into study sheets, and record and average my grades to ensure that I achieve a minimum average grade of 93% and final grade of A as listed on my transcript so that I can make dean's list, gain acceptance into grad school, maintain my student loan, and stick it to my brother.

EXERCISE 6.4

Monitoring My Success

Directions: The establishment of SMART goals provides the beacon that you can use to keep on track and monitor your progress. Accomplishing your goals is something to celebrate; it is also an experience that you want to repeat. This exercise invites you to review your goals, your level of achievement, and what you did to get to this level of success. The last column provides you with direction regarding what you want to continue to do as well as what you may want to adjust.

Goal	How I did—the good, bad, and ugly	What I did to achieve this goal (do I repeat or adjust?)

TIME MANAGEMENT

Have you ever found yourself bleary-eyed and strung out from too much coffee and too little sleep after pulling an "all-nighter" right before the big biology test? Or maybe you had the experience of panicking when you remembered that the 20-page paper you were assigned the first day of class is due by the next lesson. If these or other similar examples of poor planning are familiar, then learning to improve your skills with time management may be what you need.

As a college student, you are presented with numerous assignments and demands. The truth is that there are only 24 hours in a day to accomplish all that is on your plate. But another fact is that others face similar tasks and the same time-limited resources of 24 hours. The question, therefore, is how do they do it? How do they do it so efficiently and effectively? The answer? They have excellent time management skills.

Not only do people who possess excellent time management skills accomplish more, but they tend to be the highest achievers. It is not that they work harder, although that is a real possibility; good time managers work smarter.

Since you can't create more time, it makes sense to develop the skills needed to manage the time you have so that you can accomplish all you wish to do effectively and efficiently.

7.1: The "What" of Time Management

Time management is the process of planning and exercising conscious control over the allocation of your time between the various demands you are encountering. Your current focus is most likely on managing the time you need to be successful at your online course. Your course, however, isn't the only thing in your life. Successful time management will require you to make choices about how you will allocate your time and energy across various domains of your life, including your education, family life, social life, physical needs, and even personal interests and hobbies. Having a realistic view of all of the demands on your time as well as a real sense of the energy available to you will be essential to the planning and organization that is key to time management.

7.2: The "Why" of Time Management

Individuals who employ sound time management skills accomplish more with less effort. The ability to control time allocation to tasks improves your ability to focus and thus enhances your efficiency. Time management also contributes to improved decision-making by reducing the number of times you jump to conclusions without fully considering all options because of a time crunch. With proper time management skills, you will feel less rushed, overwhelmed, and stressed. The effectiveness and efficiency that results from good time management not only creates more confidence but will help you prevent the dreaded "I'll do it later" mentality of procrastination. Finally, time management skills also enable you to attend to all aspects of your life—including those that allow you to relax and unwind. Additional benefits to effective time management are listed in Table 7.1.

Table 7.1. Benefits of Good Time Management

• Higher productivity and efficiency • Less stress • Greater balance in life • Meeting time-sensitive goals • Increased efficiency in workflow • Increased work quality

7.3: Time Bandits

Increasing your effectiveness and efficiency will require you to not only develop a time management skill set but also control conditions that are time bandits, robbing you of this limited resource at a time when you need it most. It can be too easy to allow yourself to be pulled away from the online lesson or unit that you intended to do and instead start surfing the web, browsing social media sites, or maybe signing on to an Internet game. These are time bandits that need to be avoided. One strategy is to use these activities as rewards for completing a little chunk of the assigned online work. While the distraction of attractive alternative activities is a time bandit that needs to be controlled, there are others. Exercise 7.1 identifies several of these "bandits" along with suggestions for "arresting" them. Your task is to identify those that challenge you and develop your plan for arresting (and removing) them.

EXERCISE 7.1

"Arresting" the "Time Bandits"

Directions: After reviewing the conditions that can interfere with your effective use of time and the suggestions provided, develop your plan for those "bandits" that you experience.

Time bandit	Suggestion to "arrest"	Your plan?
Feeling so overwhelmed that one seeks to avoid rather than attack	1. Set priorities. 2. Challenge your thinking if you are catastrophizing the possible negative impact of a less-than-perfect outcome.	

(Continued)

Time bandit	Suggestion to "arrest"	Your plan?
Doubt that I can do it; spend more time thinking/ rethinking and doubting	1. Take a moment to remember the exception to this situation. That is, remember a time when you were successful in a similar situation. 2. Break up work into as many small, achievable tasks as you can. 2. Commit to one small step.	
Spinning wheels—with little progress	1. Prioritize … prioritize … prioritize. Refocus on tasks that are relevant. 2. Start with an activity that has the least cost (in terms of time and effort) and yet a good payoff (e.g., grade, personal satisfaction).	
Distracted (daydreaming, responding to other stimuli, etc.)	1. Review your preferred learning style. Change the time of day for tackling challenging tasks. 2. Take breaks and move after completing part of the task.	
Perfectionism— why start if I don't have the perfect amount of time to get the task perfectly completed?	1. Permit yourself to do a draft and then decide if you want to revisit and revise. 2. Do a reality check. What else is going on in your life? 3. Ask yourself, will a just okay product (i.e., less than perfect) be a big deal in a week? Month? Next semester?	
Why bother— I hate this course (assignment, task)	1. Review your goals. Remind yourself of the value of moving through this course or assignment. 2. Develop a strategy to reduce the cost of completing the course or assignment while maximizing the payoff. 3. Use extrinsic motivation to move through the task. Reward yourself after each small step.	

7.4: The "How" of Time Management

Regardless of your previous experience with time management, your skills can be improved. This improvement starts with understanding the factors that contribute to the most efficient and effective use of your time and developing a time management system using the methods listed below.

As you review the description of the methods to include in a time management system, you are invited to maintain a list of how you will employ these strategies. Exercise 7.2 provides you with a checklist to help guide your time management planning. As you read through the various elements of effective time management, identify how you will use the information described to improve your time management.

EXERCISE 7.2

My Time Management Plan

Directions: For each of the strategies identified as contributing to effective time management, develop a clear, specific statement as to how you will employ that strategy as you navigate your online course.

Strategy	My Plan
Prioritize (Eisenhower model)	
Create a to-do list	
Eliminate the unnecessary and the time bandits	
Take time to set or remember your overall goals and those specific to this unit or lesson	
Develop a plan (be realistic given your current resources)	
Get organized	
Where to start? (How does each to-do item match your current state and interest?)	
How to proceed (remember breaks)	
Make it a ritual—your routine	

Prioritize

Perhaps you are a "list maker." As discussed later in this chapter, making lists, establishing schedules, and using calendars can be a useful strategy when attempting to manage your time. However, making lists which are simply a compilation of all that you wish to accomplish without determining which tasks are urgent and vital—and which tasks are less so—can be more of a time waster than no list at all.

A rigid adherence to creating and engaging with task lists may result in spending more time reviewing the lists and wasting time on unimportant activities than on completing the necessary tasks.

This is not to suggest that you should not make a list of things to do or even multiple lists. The problem that often arises is that the sheer magnitude of the things randomly written on a list can create stress and anxiety, both conditions that invite you to close your eyes and walk away. The productive to-do list is one that provides prioritization.

One model that has been used to organize tasks along a prioritization continuum is what has been called the Eisenhower model, named after President Eisenhower. The model categorizes tasks along two dimensions: importance and urgency (see Figure 7.1).

The items that you place in the first quadrant, the important and urgent quadrant, are those that you feel need to be done immediately. While these are not urgent crises, they are tasks for which you have very little wiggle room in relationship to time delay. Quadrant two, the important but not urgent items, require you to establish an end date and perhaps create calendar reminders as the date approaches. In the last two quadrants are the tasks that you have identified as unimportant. One group, unimportant yet urgent, contains things that have an impending due date but for which you feel little emotional involvement. Things such as setting up a meeting or having your group presentation emailed to the instructor are things that you don't have to do personally and could be delegated. The final quadrant contains those things which you now see are neither urgent nor important. Items in this last category, unimportant and not urgent, can be significant time wasters if they if not recognized as such or if misunderstood as more important and urgent than they are.

In addition to looking at importance and urgency as you prioritize your tasks, consider the degree to which each task is fixed or whether you have

Figure 7.1 The Eisenhower Model

	Urgent	Not Urgent
Important	Final Research paper due in 3 days	Final Research paper due in 3 weeks
Not Important	Complete end of the semester course evaluation sheet (anonymous)	Write a course review on Rate-my-Professor.

some flexibility and wiggle room. If you have to sign on for a live presentation, the day and time are set. There may be tasks, however, that are flexible. For example, you may have an assignment that can be done at any point throughout the semester. In this case, use that flexibility to your advantage by placing the task in your schedule (early, middle, late) where it most easily fits.

To-Do Lists

Making a to-do list may be the all-time tried-and-true method for time management. A to-do list or task list can be very useful for effective time management. It can be effective in that it not only helps keep you focused on completing one task at a time but it also provides a little satisfaction as you cross off the item from the list. As noted above, however, if the list is just a random, endless set of tasks without clear distinction about importance or urgency, the list that could be helpful now becomes stifling and overwhelming—potentially paralyzing you.

As you create a to-do list, you may find it useful to create a general task list and timeline for everything that needs to be accomplished throughout the semester. With this as a framework, create a weekly (or even daily) to-do list that reflects chunks of items in your general timeline that will be addressed during this specific time frame.

Whether it is a semester, a monthly, a weekly, or even a daily list, the items must be listed in a prioritized form. It is also vital that the creation of the list or lists does not take more time, energy, and attention than completing the tasks themselves.

One final point to remember is that, despite all of your planning and to-do lists, life is not totally under your control. When making a list, remember to remain flexible. Things will happen that interfere with completing your to-do list. Don't panic. You made a list, and you have the power to adjust it.

Control Interferences and Eliminate the Unnecessary

It may seem obvious; however, it is essential to remember that to be most efficient and effective, you need to eliminate any demand on your time and energy that is irrelevant and unnecessary for reaching your goals. So if your goal is to read a chapter, then taking 10 minutes to check Facebook is an unnecessary time bandit. If you are working on a paper and have committed to doing so for 30 minutes, then turn off your phone. Answering calls, checking emails, and texting are all useful in their own right, but they are unnecessary in service of reading a chapter or writing a paper.

As you structure to remove the unnecessary, you also want to establish a structure that will reduce interruptions. When you are working online, others may misinterpret the situation as something that they are free to interrupt. You are at work, and they would not typically interrupt if they knew that. It is helpful to establish a routine that helps you transition from relaxing and being social to engaging intellectually with your work as a student. Let your roommates or family members understand that routine and be able to recognize that you have transitioned and are now in a "please do not disturb" phase.

Identify Goal(s)

You know the value of setting goals (see Chapter 6) to guide your overall approach to your course or an assignment, but setting goals for each session of your online course is also helpful. Creating a list that motivates you to cross off the tasks listed may be a beneficial goal for any one day or any one session. But take a moment before starting on your course and see if there is something else you wish to accomplish. Highlight your goals for this class or this one session and allow them not only to structure your plan of attack (see below) but to maintain your motivation and monitor your progress.

Develop a Plan

Understanding both your starting point and your desired ending point will invite you to consider strategies that will get you from start to finish. As you start your class, or as you begin any one session or unit, it would be essential to take five or ten minutes to take stock of the moment. Identify what it is you wish to achieve (set a small goal) and then, with this as your beacon, develop the specific steps you will take to get to that goal.

In developing your plan, you may be tempted to multitask, thinking that more is better. It is not. It is more efficient and more productive to work on one task, giving it your full attention.

Get Organized

Organization is a super contributor to efficient time management. Clear up the clutter in your work area and try to develop a sound filing system to maintain all your materials. Develop the habit of filing away things in some clear, logical categories immediately after you have used them. Organization can reduce time wasted hunting for things you need and thus free up time to focus on completing the task at hand.

Where to Start

With your list of priorities and things to do, you still need to think about where to start. If the tasks you are trying to accomplish are scaffolded—that is, one builds on the next—then clearly the hierarchy needs to guide your decisions about where to start and how to proceed. When just a general structure exists, reflect on the tasks as they run in concert with how you are feeling at the moment. Are you focused? Then target reading and studying. Are you feeling creative? Then begin on the paper or the project that you need to do. Are you a bit tired, struggling to get moving? In this situation, find a small task or a task that can be easily broken into smaller segments.

How to Proceed

Hopefully, as you get into your work, you will also get into a flow, where progress is being made and awareness of time spent may be lost. Even at a time like this where your productivity and efficiency are up, it is vital to take a break. When you take regular, short breaks, you will not only find that you return somewhat renewed but that you have allowed the time necessary to condense and absorb the information you just processed.

If you are the type of person that can lose all sense of time spent on a task, you may do well using a timer to remind you to take a break. Working intensely for 30 or 40 minutes, followed by a 5- or 10-minute break, will serve you well. During your break move away from the screen. Get up, move, and, if you desire, find something for a snack. Your body needs to stretch, and your mind needs to rest.

Make This All a No Brainer

Just thinking about all of these steps in time management can be exhausting. It may feel entirely artificial in the beginning, especially if all of these suggestions are foreign to your typical approach to task management. The good news is that with repetition each of these steps will become a habit. Over time you will find that these elements fall in place as your ritual for attacking self-directed learning.

TASK MANAGEMENT

Have you ever looked at a syllabus and the course requirements and felt like there was no way you would ever get all of it done? If so, you are not alone. The difficulty with successfully completing the work you are assigned might be compounded by the fact that an online course may demand reliance on your own abilities to organize, structure, plan, and motivate your self-directed learning.

Learning to organize and plan your actions into outcomes and tasks leading to those outcomes over a designated period is the essence of task management. The ability to manage the tasks you are assigned is a vital skill for succeeding, not only at this one course or one program but for those tasks you will confront in life.

8.1: Task Management: The "What"

Task management is a process where one identifies and monitors the progress of work that needs to be done during a specific period of time, be that a day, a week, or a semester. For example, prior to attacking this chapter, I developed an outline of the topics I wanted to cover and identified a process for researching the overall topic of task management and the specifics such as "what," "why," and "how." In addition to setting my goals, I set a flexible timeline that I used to monitor my progress. This process of task setting and monitoring is the essence of task management.

8.2: The "Why" of Task Management

If you are like most, you probably have a kazillion things to do each day (okay maybe a little less than a kazillion). Now, not all of these things have the same level of importance, and in Chapter 6 we discussed the Eisenhower model for prioritizing.

However, even with prioritizing, you will find that multiple things seem to call for your attention all at the same time. Task management skills will help you to effectively and efficiently complete the tasks you choose to attack.

Without a systematic approach to managing the task calling for your attention, there is a real possibility that you will respond to the "loudest" or the one in your face even when it may not be the most important or valuable. Somehow the text message that just "pinged in" pulled you away from the chapter you were about to read. The text, especially once you noticed the name of sender, was clearly not a priority—but it was loud and proud and hard to resist. Perhaps engaging with one text is not that damaging. But when one text leads to another and then leads to accepting an invitation to go online to engage in a game, we may have a slight problem. Remember that chapter?

Without task management skills you may find yourself starting, stopping, and then starting again, and even abandoning what you started to try some other task. Attacking your work without a task management plan is not the most efficient or effective way to get the job done.

8.3: The "How" of Task Management

There is a very wise proverb that says, "Nothing succeeds like a deadline." This proverb is especially pertinent to the manner in which we organize our plan of action into the outcomes (*Events*) and tasks (*Activity*) leading to those outcomes over a designated period of *Time*. Integrating these three variables—events, activity, and time—is critical for your task to be completed efficiently and effectively.

When developing a task management plan consider each of the following.

1. Know What You Need to Do.

Know When Things Are Due.

As a good first step to developing your system of task management, you should take an inventory of everything you need to do. That means everything.

I know we are focusing on your education and the demands of an online course, but your education does not occur in a bubble outside of the demands of life. As such, the list you make should be an exhaustive list. Include everything from completing a paper to cleaning your room or making a family dinner.

It is important to identify and list all of the demands since they will all require your time, your energy, and your attention at some level. When possible, identify the date or deadline that is associated with each task. If no deadline is assigned, place your preferred date next to the item.

Yikes, looking at the list may begin to seem overwhelming. Guess what? If it is overwhelming on paper, it must be suffocating to keep it all jammed into your brain. Making a list of all the things that you have been thinking about allows you to "dump your brain" so that these items are not constantly spinning up into consciousness. Also, seeing all the items listed on paper will make it easier to prioritize (see Chapter 7) and allow you to separate the "urgent" items from the "someday" items.

2. Any Discretionary Time?

As you identify the "have to" items on your priority list, it is important to assign them a place in your calendar. Before putting them into the calendar, take a moment to see if they are really must do's or if they can be done in some abbreviated form (just a little start) or even moved to another time.

Once you identify these committed times, try to keep that sacred. Block them off and commit to not moving or adjusting unless something of extraordinary importance needs to be addressed. With your calendar getting filled pretty rapidly it is important to remember that you do have and do need to have a life outside of schoolwork. Rather than simply allowing things to fall by the wayside or randomly intrude on your calendar, take a moment to list activities that renew your energy. Write in "tasks" to visit friends, exercise, play, or simply put your feet up and relax. It may seem silly to plan such tasks. It is not. Without planning, you may either forget to engage in these life-renewing activities or allow them to intrude too much and interfere with your academic tasks. The idea is to balance all the tasks and manage each in way that maximizes your success and satisfaction.

3. Select the Task to Attack.

Now that you have 'brain dumped' and created a pretty exhaustive list of tasks that need your attention, it is time to prune your list and reconsider your priorities. With this processes complete, select the task that you wish to attack, and let's begin planning that attack.

4. Develop a Task Management Plan.

Understanding the nature of task management and having a prioritized list of the tasks to attack leads to the next step: engage in a method of management. There are various methods offered in the research for structuring and engaging in task management. One method which has been used since the early 1950s is the Program Evaluation Review Technique or PERT (Cook, 1966), which is described below.

8.4: The Program Evaluation Review Technique (PERT)

The PERT methodology for planning and organizing change was first developed by the U.S. Navy in the 1950s to organize and coordinate the submarine missile program. Key to this method, as well as most other models, is that the task management process requires establishing a starting point, depicting a measurable end point (i.e., outcome objective), identifying tasks (i.e., activities) that lead to sub-goals, and establishing a specific time frame.

The task management plan, one resulting in the achievement of the desired outcome, will be a depiction of a chain with each link representing the sub-goals, the tasks, and the time required to achieve those sub-goals. This approach will allow you to take a major project or a complex task and break it down into discrete parts that are interconnected and can be arranged in a logical sequence. Knowing what step A is, and that it leads to step B and so on, provides the necessary structure to help you stay on task and make progress.

When budgeting your time for any complex task, it is important to know the due date. Knowing the nature of the product or outcome and the date that production is needed will help in creating the actual linked chain of events found in a PERT chart (Cook, 1966).

One approach to developing this chart for task management would be to work backwards from the final due date to the present, taking note of marker points by which you would want to have completed various portions of the task. In the case of completing a research paper, for example, you may list (in reverse order) turning the paper in, printing the paper, final draft, making edits, producing a draft, developing an outline, researching, deciding on a topic, and understanding the assignment requirements and scoring rubric.

Planning backwards in time can help you get a feel for what is realistically possible and will help you avoid last-minute time crunches. This process is not restricted to complex or complicated academic or work tasks. In fact you have probably used a similar approach, perhaps unknowingly, when engaging with social activities. For example, imagine that you were going to go to party with some friends and you are picking them up. Knowing when you wanted (or expected) to arrive at the party, along with the locations and driving times to each of your friend's houses, you could identify when you should take your shower and get ready. This is good task management.

While such a method may not need to be written out when applied to these more typical social or personal events, you may find that writing out the timeline will be a stress buster for moderately difficult and elongated time frames.

Figure 8.1 presents a simple PERT chart for creating and delivering a major class presentation. In this PERT chart you will see all of the components necessary for planning and organizing the presentation.

The student in this illustration began by framing the ends of the horizontal line with the starting point on the left and the end state, the end of the actual presentation, on the right. The sequence of sub-goals (products or events) was then placed below the line. The illustration identifies the sub-goals by assigning a letter (as identification label) to each sub-goal. This allows the student to then return to each sub-goal and identify the steps and resources needed to accomplish that sub-goal.

Figure 8.1. Sample PERT Chart—Classroom Presentation

Starting							Project
Present							Complete
12/20/20	1/3	2/5	3/3	3/20	4/1/20	4/4	4/10

First class **A** Topic **B** Gather **C** Select **D** Design **E** Rehearse **F** Gather **G** Class presentation

received   Approval   Research   Materials   Power   Presentation materials

assignment   Articles   for slides   point slides

Tasks to move From "A" to "G"

A to B:

1. Review syllabus to identify everything that will need to be done
2. Review the Power Point class presentation assignment description and grading rubric
3. Review acceptable topics
4. Do a quick search on a couple of topics that seem interesting
5. Select two topics that seem most interesting
6. Email professor to ask for approval of my first or second choice
7. Following professor response (if accepted) move to "B" if rejected revisit tasks in "A"

A chain of sub-goals and contingent steps can be created by working from either end of the continuum. If the student in the illustration (Figure 8.1) started at the beginning, dated January 20, 2020, attempting to move from what is designated sub-task A (understanding course requirements) to sub-task B (gaining approval for project topic), she would engage in a number of steps, all listed in the illustration. These steps would include (a) reviewing course requirements, (b) reviewing the specific presentation assignment requirements, (c) considering possible topics, etc. Each succeeding sub-goal of the next link in the chain would be identified, and the specific actions needed to move from B to C and so on would be listed. This approach is considered forward chaining.

An alternative to forward chaining is when the student starts planning at the finish line (having completed the presentation) and builds her event line from right to left. Through backward chaining she would identify the event that would precede but directly lead to her desired goal, which in this illustration would be the presentation of her project to the class. So for our illustration we could imagine that the step immediately preceding her presenting the material may have included having her PowerPoint on a thumb drive and a laptop connected and operating with the projection system. She would continue this process until she arrived at her starting point, January 20, 2020.

The advantage of backward chaining is that you can use each sub-goal event as the reference for determining the immediate antecedent condition. Exercise 8.1 invites you to use the illustration provided (Figure 8.1) and give it a try. You don't have to pick a school project to get a feel for this process. If you prefer, think about a personal project that you would like to tackle, maybe organizing your room, planning for a vacation, fixing a car. Any project that will require a sequence of activities and to which you can assign a timeline will work.

My PERT Chart

Directions: Identify an academic or personal project that you wish to or need to achieve within a specific timeline. Using the illustration provided as your model (a) identify the project by name, (b) describe your starting and finishing points, and (c) determine the sub-goals and time assigned to complete each sub-goal.

With the PERT established, review what will be needed in terms of resources and activities to move from sub-goal to sub-goal. List those separately as illustrated in our example.

8.5: Task Management for Group Projects

It is very likely that you will be assigned a group project at some point in your educational career. Group projects can be a very valuable experience. In addition to gaining the additional resources of a peer, working on group projects invites you to learn to collaborate as a team, distribute responsibilities, develop communication networks, and produce a product that is better than something that any one of the individuals in the group could have produced … assuming that the group is a well-functioning group and that appropriate task management strategies are in place.

When managing a group project, one of the biggest challenges is to make sure that everyone is doing the tasks assigned within the timeline agreed upon. One task management approach for group work in various settings and organizations is developing a Gantt chart.

A Gantt chart is simply a timeline of your project. It's a tool that helps you manage all of the different resources, people, and tasks along the way to accomplishing the goal of your project. Gantt charts may seem complicated at first, and they can be (see Figure 8.2).

Fortunately, you can make them as simple or as elaborate as you wish, and there are many free and low-cost software programs available to help

Figure 8.2. Illustration of a Gantt Chart for a Graduate Class Project

EDC 571 Theories of Counseling Application Project

Members: M. Broderick, R. Smithe , N.Zhang, J. Ortez

Start: Wed. 4/6/2020 **Presentation:** May 4

Task	Assigned to	Progress	Start date	End Date	April 4	April 11	April 18	April 25	May 4
Decide on theory	Group	100%	April 6	April 6	Finished				
Assign research areas	Group	100%	April 6	April 6	Finished				
Share research upload google doc	Each member	100%	April 7	April 18	Finished				
Agree on articles to use	Group	100%	April 20	April 20					
First draft of paper	Naijian and Mary	50%	April 21	April 25			Finished		
Draft of power point with voice overs (use research bullets)	Jose and Richard	75%	April 21	April 28					
Tweak paper	Jose and Richard		April 26	April 28					
Tweak PP	Naijian and Mary		April 28	May 1					
Class presentation practice (assign roles)	Group		May 2	May 2					
Final presentation	Group		May 4	May 4					

Legend: finished | dates not used | in process | time to complete you (see added resources). But without getting too grandiose, a simple Gantt chart would have the following fundamental components:

Task names: When you receive a group project, there will be a number of related steps or tasks that will need to be organized. For example, as a group you will have to decide on the topic you will work on, begin researching the topic, develop a draft of the presentation, and then revise and finalize your work prior to the actual presentation. This information runs vertically down the left of the Gantt chart, describes project work, and may be organized into groups and subgroups.

Dates: Each task will be assigned a starting date and a completion due date. This information runs horizontally across the top of the Gantt chart and shows months, weeks, days, and years. These dates, when placed in a spreadsheet, can then be translated into the length of work (duration) to be assigned to each task.

Progress: Shows how far along the work is and may be indicated by *% Complete* and/or bar shading.

Resource assigned: Indicates the person or team responsible for completing a task.

Whether you choose to develop a formal Gantt chart or simply use an old pen and pencil approach to develop your own visual chart, it is helpful to lay out a task list with a time line and the person assigned. If each member of your team agrees to the plan—and the use of the visual chart as their reminder—you will find the group project to be a lot less stressful and much more successful.

FINAL THOUGHTS

The research suggests that online courses and programs are the wave of the future. So if you are currently enrolled in an online course, count yourself as a trailblazer.

As noted throughout this book, the online experience can be quite freeing. It is, in most cases, a delivery system that allows you to engage with the learning material in a way that maximizes your academic success and personal satisfaction. But, also as noted, the structure (or limited structure) provided by most online courses will require you to take more personal responsibility for managing your time, your energies, and your attendance to the tasks assigned. This experience truly will tap your ability to be a self-directed learner.

Success at employing the techniques described within this book will not only serve you well in this one academic experience but will position you to be a truly self-directed, self-managed, and self-regulated individual. All of these skills will position you for success in life.

So, best wishes on your continued growth and your academic success.

RP/2020

APPENDIX

WHERE TO TURN— ADDITIONAL RESOURCES

In Print

Allen, D. (2015). *Getting Things Done: The Art of Stress-Free Productivity.* New York, NY: Penguin Publishing.

Allen, D. (2019). *The Getting Things Done Workbook.* New York, NY: Penguin Books.

Allen, K., Sheve, J., & Nieter, V. (2010). *Understanding Learning Styles: Making a Difference for Diverse Learners.* Huntington Beach, CA: Shell Education.

Bandura, A. (1997). *Self-Efficacy: The Exercise of Control.* New York, NY: MacMillan.

Barrett, J. (2019). *Strategies & Tips for Time Management.* Kindle Version, Author.

Blair, G. R. (n.d.). *Goal Setting 101: An Easy, Step-by-Step Guide for Setting and Achieving a Goal.* Palm Harbor, FL: GoalsGuy Learning Systems, Inc.

Boyd, D. (2004). The characteristics of successful online students. *New Horizons in Adult Education and Human Resource Development, 18*(2), 31–39.

Budhair, S. S., & Skipwith, K. (2017). *Best Practices in Engaging Online Learners Through Active and Experiential Learning Strategies.* London: Routledge.

Cleary, T. J. (2018). *The Self-Regulated Learning Guide.* New York, NY: Routledge.

Dembo, M. H., & Seli, H. (2020). *Motivation and Learning Strategies for College Success: A Focus on Self-Regulated Learning* (6th ed.). New York, NY: Routledge.

Ellis, K. (1998). *Goal Setting for People Who Hate Setting Goals.* New York, NY: Three Rivers Press.

Gilkey, C. (2019). *Start Finishing: How to Go from Idea to Done.* Kindle Version, Author.

Harasim, L. (2017). *Learning Theory and Online Technologies.* London: Routledge.

Knoblauch, M. (2018). *The Art of Efficiency: A Guide for Improving Tax Management in the Home to Help Maximize Your Leisure Time.* Kindle Edition.

Kogan, K., & Blakemore, S. (2015). *Project Management for the Unofficial Project Manager*. Dallas, TX: BenBella Books, Inc.

Markway, B., & Ampel, C. (2018). *A Guide to Overcoming Self-Doubt and Improving Self-Esteem*. Emeryville, CA: Althea Press.

Peterson, K., & Kolb, D. A. (2017). *How You Learn Is How You Live*. San Francisco, CA: Berrett-Koehler, Publications, Inc.

Schrum, L. & Hong, S. (2002). Dimensions and strategies for online success: Voices from experienced educators. *Journal of Asynchronous Learning Networks, 6*(1), 57–67.

Smith, D. K. (1999). *Make Success Measurable!: A Mindbook-Workbook for Setting Goals and Taking Action*. New York, NY: John Wiley & Sons.

Web-Based

Bandura, A. (1977). Self-efficacy: Toward a unifying theory for behavioral change. *Psychological Review, 84*, 191–215. https://doi.org/10.1037/0033-295X.84.2.191

Donovan, J. (2015, October 8). *The importance of building online learning communities*. Colorado State University. http://blog.online.colostate.edu/blog/online-education/the-importance-of-building-online-learning-communities/

Education Planner. *What's your learning style? 20 questions*. http://www.education-planner.org/students/self-assessments/learning-styles-quiz.shtml (20-question learning style inventory).

Johnson, V. (2010, February 16). *Jim Rohn setting goals part 1* [Video]. YouTube. http://www.youtube.com/watch?v=YuObJcgfSQA

Johnson, V. (2010, April 5). *Jim Rohn setting goals part 2* [Video]. YouTube. http://www.youtube.com/watch?v=kmM_XkxuCxY&NR=1

Juenja, P. (2019). *Time management—meaning and its importance*. Management Study Guide. https://www.managementstudyguide.com/time-management.htm

Kuypers, L. (n.d.). *The zones of regulation*. Kuypers Consulting, Inc. http://www.zonesofregulation.com/index.html

LaRocca, B. (2017, April 15). *Self-efficacy tool kit*. Transforming education. https://www.transformingeducation.org/self-efficacy-toolkit/

Learning-styles-online. *Free learning styles inventory, including graphical results*. https://www.learning-styles-online.com/inventory/ (70-question learning style inventory).

Lemmo, J. (2020, February 19). *16 resources to help your students develop self regulation skills*. Everfi. https://everfi.com/insights/blog/16-resources-to-help-your-students-develop-self-regulation-skills/

Lineham, N. (2016). *Productivity & time management: The Pareto principle*. People HR. https://www.peoplehr.com/blog/2016/05/24/productivity-time-management-the-pareto-principle/

Microsoft. (n.d.). *Simple Gantt chart*. https://templates.office.com/en-us/simple-gantt-chart-tm16400962

Minnesota State University, Mankato. (2011). *Online learning considerations.* https://mankato.mnsu.edu/academics/online-and-off-campus-programs/online-education/online-learning-considerations/https://goo.gl/SDhgnW

Norman, S. (2016). *5 advantages of online learning: Education without leaving home.* eLearning Industry. https://goo.gl/jzzyUV

Office timeline. (n.d.). *How to make a Gantt chart in Excel.* https://www.officetimeline.com/make-gantt-chart/excel (free software for Gantt charting).

O'Malley, S. (2017). *Professors share ideas for building community in online courses.* Inside Higher Ed. https://www.insidehighered.com/digital-learning/article/2017/07/26/ideas-building-online-community

Solution Tree Press. (2010). *Why do we need SMART goals?* West Virginia Department of Education. https://wvde.state.wv.us/ctn/Research/whydowe-needsmartgoals.pdf

Stone, K. (2016). *Building community in online courses.* American Association for Adult and Continuing Education. http://www.aaace.org/news/272788/Building-Community-in-Online-Courses.htm

Team Gantt. (n.d.). *What is a Gantt chart?* https://www.teamgantt.com/what-is-a-gantt-chart

University of Connecticut. *An introduction to self-efficacy.* https://nrcgt.uconn.edu/underachievement_study/self-efficacy/se_section1/

REFERENCES

Alexander, M. W., Truell A. D., & Zhao, J. J. (2012). Expected advantages and disadvantages of online learning. *Issues in Information Systems, 13*(2), 193–200.

Babson Study: Over 7.1 Million Higher Ed Students Learning Online. (n.d.). Retrieved November 23, 2014, https://www.babson.edu/about/news-events/babson-announcements/babson-survey-study-of-online-learning/

Bandura, A. (2005). Evolution of social cognitive theory. In K. G. Smith & M. A. Hitt (Eds.), *Great minds in management* (pp. 9–35). Oxford University Press.

Berg, I. K., & Miller, S. D. (1992). *Working with the problem drinker: A solution-focused approach.* W. W. Norton & Company.

Chaney, E. G. (2001). Web-based instructions in a rural high school: A collaborative inquiry into its effectiveness and desirability. *NASSP Bulletin, 85*(628), 20–35.

Cook, D.L. (1966). *Program evaluation and review techniques: Application in Education* (Monograph No. 17). Washington, D.C.: U.S. Office of Education, Office of Education Cooperative Research.

Dunn, R. (2000). Learning styles: Theory, research, and practice. *National Forum of Applied Educational Research Journal, 13*(1), 3–22.

Dweck, C. (2006). *Mindset: The new psychology of success.* Ballantine Books.

Fleming, N., & Baume, D. (2006). Learning styles again: VARKing up the right tree! *Educational Developments, 7.4,* 4–7.

Matuga, J. M. (2009). Self-regulation, goal orientation, and academic achievement of secondary students in online university courses. *Journal of Educational Technology & Society, 12*(3), 4–11. http://search.proquest.com/docview/1287037464?accountid=277700

National Center for Education Statistics. (2014). Enrollment in distance education courses, by state: Fall 2012. https://nces.ed.gov/pubs2014/2014023.pdf

You, J., & Kang, M. (2014). The role of academic emotions in relationship between perceived academic control and self-regulated learning in online learning. *Computers & Education, 77,* 125–133.

Zimmerman, B. J. (2000). Attaining self-regulation: A social cognitive perspective. In M. Boekaerts, P. R. Pintrich., & M. Zeidner (Eds.), *Handbook of self-regulation* (pp. 13–41). Academic Press.

Zimmerman, B. J. (2011). Motivational sources and outcomes of self-regulated learning and performance. In B. J. Zimmerman & D. H. Schunk (Eds.), *Handbook of self-regulation of learning and performance* (pp. 49–64). Routledge.